THE ENIGMA STORY

THE ENIGMA STORY

THE TRUTH BEHIND THE 'UNBREAKABLE' WORLD WAR II CIPHER

DERMOT TURING

This edition published in 2022 by Arcturus Publishing Limited
26/27 Bickels Yard, 151–153 Bermondsey Street,
London SE1 3HA

AD008865UK

Printed in the UK

Contents

From the time of Caesar

It is sometimes said that war is the father of all things. Whether that is true or not, the Enigma cipher machine may fairly claim to have been begotten out of a style of warfare created for the twentieth century during World War I. Although our impressions of that conflict are rooted in trenches and attrition, ultimately overcome through the invention of tanks and air combat, the greatest innovation may have been in the style of command. Generals and admirals began the war recognizing that they could control huge forces spread over much greater areas than before, through the new communications medium of wireless telegraphy.

It is one of the mysteries of the universe that, although radio waves travel in straight lines, they can wrap around the earth's surface or bounce off the ionosphere, depending on atmospheric conditions, and this enabled those World War I generals and admirals to communicate effectively with units far distant from their own headquarters. A new breed of signals staff was needed to cope with the idiosyncratic behaviour of the airwaves – and to keep the wireless signals secure. For in the earliest days of World War I the German Army had achieved a momentous victory against Imperial Russia, simply because the Russians broadcast their orders in plain language for anyone to hear. The need for codes and ciphers could not have been more urgent.

Assisting on the fringes of the conflict was an engineer and inventor called Dr Arthur Scherbius. He was born in Frankfurt in 1878, and already had a number of patents under his belt by the time war broke out. His inventions mainly concerned electrical motors, though it is clear that his imagination ranged more widely. In 1915, Scherbius found himself teaching wireless telegraphy in the Kaiser's army, and by 1917 in the newly-established Weapons and Munitions Procurement Office, which was instructed by the War Ministry to develop a cipher device which might carry out the task of message concealment by some mechanical method. Around this time, Scherbius started to think about how a cipher machine might be developed.

Codes and ciphers have been around since the earliest times. Julius Caesar is supposed to have used a very simple form of cipher, in which each letter in the alphabet is represented by a different one, shifted three letters on. So, the words 'Veni, vidi, vici' would have been enciphered as 'Zhqm, zmgm, zmfm', which ought to have been enough to confuse even Latin-speaking Britons after the Romans trampled over their country. (As the Roman alphabet had only 23 letters, the three-letter shift gives rise to some changes which might not be

Plain	A	B	C	D	E	F	G	H	I	K	L	M	N	O	P	Q	R	S	T	V	X	Y	Z
Cipher	D	E	F	G	H	J	K	L	M	N	O	P	Q	R	S	T	V	X	Y	Z	A	B	C

expected by modern Britons.) If you were unlucky enough to have a word with an X, Y or Z in it, instead of the cipher dropping off the end, you started again at the beginning, as if the cipher had been wrapped around the outside of a wheel, to get A, B or C. A Caesar-shift cipher is not particularly sophisticated and is very easily broken.

To make the Caesar idea more complicated, the number of places to shift the letters can vary according to a codeword. For example, the codeword 'Eboracum' could signify that, for the first letter to be enciphered, A shifts by +4 places to E, B shifts +4 to F, and so forth; for the second letter to be enciphered, A shifts by +1 place to B, B shifts +1 to C, and so forth; for the third letter A shifts by +13 (because of the short Roman alphabet), and so on. This adaptation of Caesar's system is named after Blaise de Vigenère, for obscure reasons because, apparently, he did not actually invent it. The Vigenère cipher is a lot more secure than Caesar's, so much so that for centuries it was called *le chiffre indéchiffrable*, or 'the unbreakable cipher'. Still, if the methodology is known then it becomes very important to keep the codeword a secret. Even if it's not known, codebreakers would have known – certainly by the time of World War I – how to discover that this type of cipher repeats the Caesar shift after every eighth letter, and to find the pattern.

A further sophistication can be added: if the substitute alphabet is randomized, it will be much harder to discern the pattern. The simple Caesar substitutions we have looked at so far all assume that the cipher alphabet is in the familiar A, B, C, D, E order, but it need not be so. Indeed, a different alphabet order could be used for each of the letters in the signal to be enciphered. In modern English there are 403-million-million-million-million possible alphabetical orders to choose from, which ought to rule out the possibility of one's opponent finding the right one by guesswork or brute force testing of each in sequence. On the other hand, it means that the recipient of the signal would need to have a book or a chart setting out which of those different alphabets is being used when, or maybe instead to be told a methodology or algorithm which explains how to identify or construct the correct alphabetical sequence for deciphering each successive letter of an encrypted signal. Of course, keeping the book or the alphabet-finding method secure is the same problem as keeping the codeword 'Eboracum' secure. Codebreakers and codemakers refer to the secret information – the book, the codeword, or whatever it is – which must at all costs be kept a secret, since the cipher technique is probably already known to the enemy as the 'key' to the cipher.

Which of these techniques to use is usually a trade-off between security and convenience. Using the book approach is best, but only if the book is used only once. Producing single-use cipher books in quantity is expensive and difficult. A key which relies on a routine or a methodology for creating the cipher alphabet is a good deal simpler and cheaper, but security depends on the method having sufficient complexity and unpredictability to foil the attacks of would-be codebreakers.

Arthur Scherbius's contribution to the complexity of cipher creation was to encapsulate a substitution alphabet into a wheel. On one circular face of the wheel would be the unenciphered alphabet, and on the other the randomly-chosen new one. Behind the surfaces of the wheel would be connections to link each plain-text letter to its substitute. The beauty of using a wheel, though, was that with each new letter in the message the wheel could spin around. So, if the substitutions made by the wheel were as follows for the first input letter:

Input letter	A	B	C	D	E
Substitute	K	A	R	Q	V

the wheel would rotate to create a new set of substitutions, shifted on one space as if following a Vigenère model:

Input letter	A	B	C	D	E
Substitute	S	K	A	R	Q

Better still, the substitute letters indicated as outputs from the wheel could be used as input letters for another cipher wheel, creating yet more randomization, which would be especially difficult to unravel if the motion of the wheels was different. With each extra wheel in the system, the number of apparently random alphabets which have to be cycled through before a repeat is reached is multiplied – in the English alphabet of 26 letters – by 26. The chances of using the codebreakers' technique of looking for repeats after so many letters should be foiled by such a system.

Scherbius's invention was simple to understand and at the same time produced ciphers of bewildering complexity: it was the perfect combination. Perhaps for this reason, since the story of Enigma became better known its origins have become fogged over with controversy: did the first idea for a rotor-based cipher machine come from the Dutch inventor Hugo Koch? Or maybe the central concepts were co-invented separately by the American Edward Hebern or the Swede Arvid Damm? The fog is thickened when it is revealed that Scherbius bought Koch's own patent, even though this was for a machine which used hydraulic, pneumatic or optical transmission rather than electrical contacts between the rotors. In the end, it probably matters little. Scherbius submitted his own patent application on 23 February 1918 for an electrical machine, in which the encipherment would be shown by illuminating small light-bulbs like those found in electric torches. This was called the 'light-bulb machine' or 'Enigma, Model A'.

Solving Enigma

The word 'enigma' is itself a puzzle with a bewildering array of solutions.

The dictionary will tell you that the word is derived from the Greek αἴνιγμα,αῐι meaning a riddle or a puzzle or a 'dark saying' – perfect for the mystery and concealment enabled by Scherbius's invention. But there's rather more to it than just a cute name for a clever machine:

- A family of beetles has been named 'Enigma'
- Sir Edward Elgar's *Enigma Variations* is said to contain encoded information, the details of which remain a musicological puzzle a century after they were composed
- Films, television shows and computer games called 'Enigma' abound, and not many of them have anything to do with cipher machines
- The writer William S. Burroughs launched a foray into numerology with his concept of the '23 Enigma', in which various curious coincidences are linked to the number 23
- The singer Lady Gaga branded a huge musical extravaganza launched in 2018 as the *Lady Gaga Enigma*, offering 'creativity and courage that is grown out of adversity, love and music'
- And there's even a town in Tennessee called Enigma.

Unfortunately for Scherbius, the war came to a crashing end, culminating in the Treaty of Versailles which cut the size of the German Army to 100,000 men and shrank its budget accordingly. For the time being, he was on his own with his invention, but he soon recognized that there might be demand for secrecy in communications in diplomacy and business as much as on the battlefield. Scherbius set to work anyway, and by 1923 he was ready to present a design to the public.

The cipher machine he actually created didn't have lightbulbs. In fact, it was very like a typewriter, with levered letter keys and a roller for paper. But if you typed on this machine, the text which appeared on the paper was not what you typed: for the act of typing closed an electrical circuit which passed through four coding rotors, each of which substituted a different output for the electrical input. The machine used a 28-character alphabet, and the rotors moved in an irregular fashion every time a letter was typed. (The extra characters may have been to signal to the reader to switch between 'alpha' and 'numeric' interpretations of the typed message, because there was no ability to type actual numbers on the machine; but the user manual does not confirm this for certain.) The rotors could be taken out of the machine and their order rearranged, and the user could select the starting-position of each of the rotors using knobs on the side of the machine. Finally, a lever at the front gave a choice between encipherment mode, decipherment mode and typewriter mode, where the encipherment mechanism was bypassed altogether so that the device behaved like a normal electric typewriter. Scherbius promoted his device in the electrical-gadgets publication *Zeitschrift für Fernmeldetechnik, Werk- und Gerätebau*.

There was just one problem: 1923 was a terrible year for the German economy. At the end of the war, a loaf of bread cost 50 pfennigs. By January 1923 the price had increased massively, to 250 marks – a 500-fold rise. But that was nothing. By November of that year, if you needed to buy bread with cash, you had to part with 201 billion marks. With the economy in disarray, nobody was going to be in the market for esoteric cipher machines.

Scherbius's old typewriting version of the Enigma machine.

Undeterred, Scherbius was able to secure a deal whereby his company sold a fistful of cipher-machine patents and prototypes to a newly-established company called Chiffriermaschinen AG, which exhibited his machine at a communications-technology event in Bern, Switzerland. Now the idea was reported on in magazines and looked into by the authorities of other countries. In August 1924 Chiffriermaschinen AG demonstrated the machine again, at the Universal Postal Congress in Stockholm, Sweden. The version on show seems to have been a more compact and transportable model than Scherbius's typewriting machine: the innovative, but heavy and cumbersome, electric-typing mechanism was replaced by the torch-bulb readout suggested in the original design, and the machine also did away with the need to switch between encipher and decipher modes. So long as sender and receiver both used the same settings, the machine was good for either operation. It was able to fit neatly into a wooden box for use on the go – ideal for military operations as well as office use. Suddenly, everyone was interested. The German Foreign Ministry looked it over for use as a security device, but conservatism ruled the day and new-fangled contraptions found no favour there. But there was interest from the Netherlands, Italy, Turkey and Japan. Even the British bought one to check it out. Finally, with adaptations to the design for added secrecy and security, in 1926 the German Army began its own tests, and the German Navy put a 29-letter version into operational use.

In May 1928 a full rollout of Enigma machines took place across the German Army. Gone were the heavy typewriting components and non-standard letters. Additional encipherment features had been added, and there were operational protocols to ensure security in use. This version of the Enigma machine was unique to the Wehrmacht, and it was destined to remain in use, with only minor modifications, up to the end of World War II.

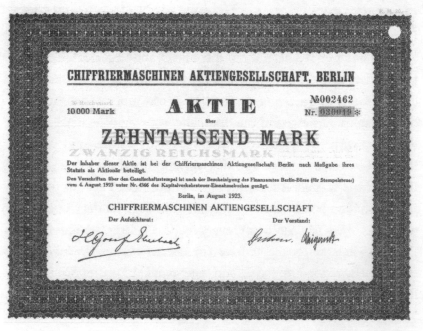

A share certificate for Scherbius's company,
showing the effect of rampant inflation.

At the core of the Wehrmacht Enigma sat the three rotors of Scherbius's vision. Twenty-six electrical contacts on the input face of each rotor were connected by wiring to 26 more on the output face. The wiring pattern inside was designed to scramble the alphabet, so that a current entering at one contact would emerge at a different position on the output face. The contacts were spring-loaded so that the emerging current entered the next rotor directly, thus moving through all three rotors for more thorough scrambling.

When it emerged from the third rotor, the current entered a 'turnaround' wheel. On the standard Wehrmacht model Enigma, this wheel did not actually rotate, but stayed in a fixed position. It had contact points only on one face, and its internal wiring ensured that a contact receiving current would be directed round to create an output at another. The turnaround wheel thus provided yet another substitution in the encipherment. (The turnaround wheel was also the clever part of the design which enabled the machine to be reciprocal – that the same settings worked for decipherment just as for encipherment, without the need to switch between 'encipher' and 'decipher' modes – and it was also the source of the codebreaker's tiny way in, that no letter could ever encipher as itself.) After leaving the turnaround wheel, the current went backwards through all three rotors, with substitutions occurring at every stage. The rotor system alone carried out seven alphabetical substitutions.

The pattern of substitutions changed with every keystroke, because pressing down on a letter brought a set of three levers called pawls into motion. These pawls pushed up on the back of the rotors, each of which was fitted with a ratchet into which the pawl could fit and move the rotor round exactly one twenty-sixth of a revolution, bringing the electrical contacts on the input and output faces of the rotor into position with different contacts on either side. However, the middle and left-hand rotors were normally prevented from engaging with their pawls by a shoulder on the right-most and middle rotors respectively. Each rotor had a notch cut into the shoulder, though, so that if the notch had moved round to the right place, on the next keystroke the adjacent rotor's pawl would be able to bite and push that adjacent rotor on. The overall effect was like the pre-digital mileage counters on older cars: the fast, right-hand rotor moved on every key-stroke, the middle rotor ordinarily moved on one step in every 26 key-strokes, and the left-most slow rotor would step on only once per complete revolution of the middle rotor.

But the Wehrmacht modification did not depend solely on the rotary system for its security. A novel feature was added to the front of the machine, which had not been seen in any of the commercially exhibited models. This was a plugboard, containing 26 dual sockets into which two-pin plugs on double-ended cables could be inserted. Any number of cables (up to the maximum of 13) could be used. The plugboard was an additional conversion device, swapping one letter for another.

So, overall, the Enigma machine carried out a remarkable number of transformations for any letter that was typed in. The first thing that happened was that the mechanical act of pressing down on a letter brought the pawls into play, moving at least one of the rotors on one place. Then the pressed-down letter closed an electrical circuit, bring the encipherment system into operation. The electricity passed first through the plugboard, and if a cable had been inserted into the socket for that letter, it would re-enter the machine's main circuitry as if a completely different letter had been pressed: if **A** had been typed, and the socket for **A** joined by a cross-plugging to **M**, from here on the machine would take it that **M** had been typed.

Next, the circuitry joined the plugboard to a circular 'entry plate' on the face of which 26 electrical contacts enabled power to reach the rotors. There was a vast number of different ways that the entry-

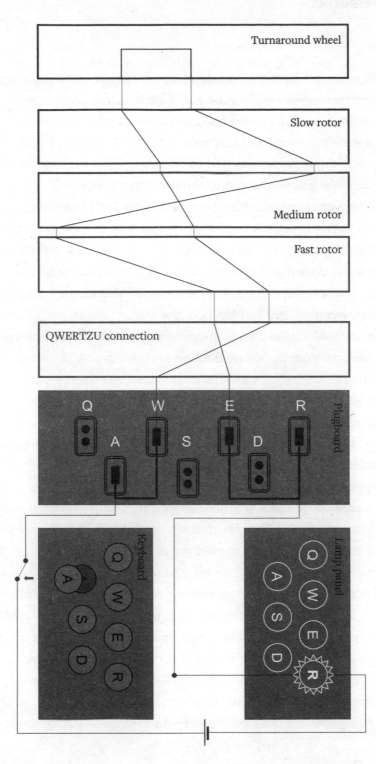

The workings of the Enigma machine.

plate contacts could be connected to the plugboard – once again 403-million-million-million-million. Which one the Wehrmacht had chosen out of this astronomical number was to become a major cryptanalytical problem for non-German codebreakers. The British, not understanding that the plugboard sat between the keyboard and the entry-plate, called it the problem of the 'QWERTZU' (after the order of letters on a standard German typewriter). The French, who were nearer the mark, called it the problem of the '*couronne fixe*', a rather attractive metaphor which visualizes the entry plate as a crown. But no amount of imaginative naming of the problem could help foreign codebreakers who, without a Wehrmacht machine in their possession, could not find out the answer as they would like to, using the well-known cryptanalytic technique called a screwdriver.

Next, the current flowed through the contacts on the rotors and the internal wiring of the rotors, the turnaround wheel, and back through the rotors to the entry plate and thence, via the mysterious QWERTZU, to the plugboard again. Depending on whether a cable was used in the socket for the exit-point letter, a further transformation might occur, and finally the circuit was completed as the electricity passed through one of the tiny light-bulbs on the lamp panel of the machine. The illuminated bulb shone through a transparent screen printed with the letters of the alphabet, showing the one letter chosen by the machine as the cipher equivalent of the letter originally typed in.

On the next key-stroke the same process would happen all over again. But now, because the first thing that happens is the stepping-on of the rotors, even if the same letter was pressed as before, the path taken by the electric current on reaching the rotors would be different. It does not preclude the possibility of the same output from the rotors, but the chance of that happening is very remote. In fact, the randomization is almost perfect – but not quite. As no letter can

A schematic drawing of the Wehrmacht version of the Enigma machine.

encipher as itself, repeatedly pressing the same key can produce a random, or near-random, sequence of 25 letters, but only 25. (Early on in World War II, at Bletchley Park, the codebreaker Mavis Lever stumbled upon a message sent by the Italian Navy enciphered on an Enigma machine, which, she observed, did not contain the letter **L** at all. She surmised that it was a practice message where the Enigma operator had just repeatedly pressed the letter **L** on his machine. It was a remarkable insight which probably helped her figure out the machine settings in use for the day, but of itself a message consisting of a string of **LLLLLLLLLLLLLL** was not of immense intelligence value.)

From the earliest days of using Enigma, the German armed forces recognized that machines might be captured on the battlefield, so that the degree of security conferred by keeping the machine and its wiring arrangements secret was limited, and probably of short duration once an actual conflict began. The answer to the battlefield capture problem was the 'key'. In the case of Enigma, the 'key' was the way the Enigma machine was to be set up; this would be changed periodically, with the settings distributed securely so that even if the key was captured the enemy would only become privy to the secret signals for a short time until the next key came into force. And the really clever thing about Enigma was the vast number of different keys that were possible.

At the start of World War II, the German Army and air force were using a version of the Enigma machine where three rotors were chosen daily from a box of five. There are 60 ways to pick and order three rotors out of five. On the rim of the rotors 26 numbers, from 01 to 26, were engraved, so that the operator could set the orientation of the rotor once it was installed in the machine. The rim itself was separate from the body of the rotor: in essence, it was a ring which could be swivelled around the body of the rotor to disguise the orientation of the rotor's internal wiring. The ring

Safety in numbers

Number of key-strokes before the cycle of alphabets repeats itself	16,900
Number of stars estimated to be in the Milky Way	between 100 and 400,000,000,000
Number of different ways to wire up the turnaround wheel	7,905,853,580,625
Number of possible substitution alphabets available from the machine, with a library of three rotors and six cross-pluggings	10,179,727,658,100,000
Number of seconds elapsed since the Universe began	432,000,000,000,000,000
Number of stars estimated to exist in the Universe	70,000,000,000,000,000,000,000
Number of different ways to wire up a rotor or the QWERTZU	403,291,461,126,605,635,584,000,000

needed to be clipped into place before the rotor was inserted into the machine. There were 26 possible positions for the ring, giving 26 × 26 × 26 options for orientating the rotor wiring on set-up. Finally, the plugboard connections needed to be made, using eight double-ended cables. The choices to be made were set out in a key table which was distributed monthly, with different tables going to different networks and units.

All of these options gave a flexible system for setting up the machine, with over 158-million-million-million settings to choose from, even with the small library of five rotors. Still, the possibility existed that the key-table for the relevant month could fall into the wrong hands. Accordingly, a further layer of concealment was used which was, by the time war broke out, specific to the individual message being sent.

Even with the three rotors (with their rings clipped into position) in the machine, it was possible to choose which of the 26 figures was uppermost on each of the rotors when encipherment of the message began. That gave 17,576 possible starting positions. Which of them had been picked was information missing from the key-sheet and, in the German Army and air force, left to the discretion of the Enigma operator, who was supposed to choose at random. There were two problems with that procedure: first, it would be necessary to tell the recipient of the message what the three rotors' starting positions were, in order to have him set up his machine the same way for deciphering; and secondly, that soldiers are human and not very good at picking figures at random. These two flaws were set to become the Achilles' heel in the whole system, providing just enough purchase for codebreakers to lever their way past the whole illusion of security being a natural consequence of very large numbers.

Arthur Scherbius did not live to see the accession of the National Socialist German Workers' Party to power and the assumption of the Chancellorship by Adolf Hitler. In May 1929, aged 50, he was involved in an accident with a horse-drawn vehicle in his company's yard, and died of his injuries. Once the Nazis took power and the remilitarization of Germany accelerated, the new means of secret communications took off as well. It is estimated that, by the time Enigma machines

GEHEIM! **SONDER MASCHINENSCHLÜSSEL** DECEMBER 1939 *May 1941*

Tag	Walzenlage			Ringstellung			Steckerverbindungen										Kenngruppen			
31	I	V	IV	01	13	04	AV	BI	CJ	DP	EM	FK	GQ	HU	SZ	TY	REJ	RFP	DNM	OAM
30	III	IV	IV	09	01	03	BV	CE	DT	FM	GS	HU	IR	JZ	KP	TW	VIV	EKX	GMA	VPG
29	V	III	I	10	08	26	AV	BG	CT	EY	FH	IW	LM	NS	OP	QR	OFR	QWE	EQR	NNN
28	III	I	IV	02	05	01	AN	BT	CL	ES	FK	HM	IR	JW	QV	YZ	BCP	ABF	GLV	ZYR
27	III	I	IV	08	01	03	AH	BV	DR	FT	JL	MN	PX	QS	UI	WZ	MYI	OTU	FZK	EKG
26	I	III	I	15	23	19	AJ	CG	DF	EK	KO	LM	PZ	QS	RX	SW	AOT	HYC	NAX	HDB
25	III	IV	IV	10	12	07	AY	BK	DN	FI	GM	HU	OW	QV	RT	XZ	FHB	UMD	VVV	DDH
24	III	I	IV	17	05	11	AB	CT	DL	FO	GW	HV	IU	JX	MR	NP	RIJ	SCN	LPE	IGW
23	II	V	II	13	23	10	AB	BG	CK	DV	FZ	JO	LW	NP	SX	TU	LPA	FKH	HJN	SBH
22	IV	IV	V	13	07	18	AR	BX	CO	EN	FL	GQ	HZ	KS	TY	UV	MTT	DUP	OZO	XVR
21	III	II	III	15	12	20	AH	BK	DS	EP	FG	IX	JU	LO	QT	WZ	MHJ	EFR	VBW	XLI
20	I	III	I	03	24	26	AO	BU	CJ	DE	GQ	HP	KW	MX	NV	ST	KPF	LJA	JBQ	EHM
19	III	II	V	22	04	24	AY	BX	FZ	GJ	HW	IU	KT	LV	OR	QS	VOH	PSZ	GHZ	CGU
18	III	IV	IV	15	14	08	AV	CI	DO	ES	FK	HY	JT	MR	PW	QX	VXM	JHM	CTR	FOK
17	II	IV	IV	01	24	11	AI	BW	CF	DT	EU	GV	JO	KP	NS	RT	AOK	COT	IXN	FOK
16	III	II	I	04	07	13	AL	BQ	DN	EI	FJ	MY	PW	RX	ST	UZ	WDU	URI	KMA	AQK
15	IV	III	IV	16	23	17	AY	BW	CG	DK	EO	FT	HJ	IX	PQ	UZ	EPH	ICM	ZHZ	PPQ
14	V	IV	V	11	15	15	AR	DU	EP	GY	IL	JV	KT	MN	OT	QU	ZCM	QZK	VDA	VJG
13	IV	IV	V	04	10	08	AL	BD	CN	FY	HX	JS	MR	OT	QU	VZ	UMJ	JXO	WPG	VSP
12	II	I	II	13	02	16	AG	BH	DW	EK	FQ	IM	LO	PZ	SV	TU	YBM	ZAX	CDW	BNN
11	III	IV	IV	02	09	20	AN	BW	CO	FL	GK	IX	MZ	PV	RT	SU	REW	EIX	RXZ	XGT
10	IV	III	II	09	09	11	AI	DM	FK	GX	JQ	LP	OR	TU	VZ	WT	FZI	AVR	VXX	HJE
09	III	II	III	05	02	22	AB	CE	DT	FG	HY	IX	JO	KV	MN	RW	COK	ABQ	MBD	YGW
08	I	V	I	25	26	06	BE	CI	DU	FK	GM	IV	JR	LO	NZ	QY	JZV	WZL	MZK	KEJ
07	V	IV	III	04	01	08	BU	CE	DS	GX	IV	KL	MT	NW	OP	QZ	OTG	LWG	WMI	HOH
06	IV	I	IV	16	19	06	AX	CE	DM	GR	HN	IO	JT	KZ	PW	UY	FUP	VSD	NRQ	IIE
05	III	IV	V	04	06	05	AZ	BH	DO	EU	FV	GR	IH	KN	LU	NX	NIL	OAQ	PHM	KWZ
04	IV	IV	I	07	12	02	AM	BQ	CR	DU	GO	HP	IT	JK	LZ	VX	WJL	QEW	VDZ	UGP
03	II	II	I	18	03	23	AH	BS	CX	DO	ER	FW	JV	LP	MZ	UY	HWJ	KBO	RLF	IWW
02	IV	III	IV	24	02	21	AY	BZ	CQ	EX	FJ	GI	KW	MS	NP	RT	HAS	NKD	CJB	MFT
01	IV	V	I	16	12	25	AU	BI	CH	DQ	EF	IO	JN	KL	MR	PW	WZA	HGK	FOB	FGM

An Enigma key-sheet.

went out of service, around 37,000 of the devices had been built. Had he lived, Scherbius might have become very rich indeed.

In 1928 the energetic Elsbeth Rinke came onto the board of Chiffriermaschinen AG. She was to become the principal commercial force behind the exploitation of the Enigma patents, her arrival being conveniently timed to match the period of expansion of Enigma machine usage. The company's technical brains were provided by Willi Korn, who is credited with having invented the turnaround wheel for the compact, reciprocal model of Enigma. In the months and years to come, the balance between profits and national security occupied increasing amounts of Mrs Rinke's time: now that the Enigma was in use throughout the German armed forces, every approach by a foreign concern seeking to buy her cipher machines needed to be vetted by the Cipher Agency in the Defence Ministry. Requests came from all over: Belgium and China (supplies not allowed); Brazil, Croatia, Ethiopia, Hungary, Iraq, Italy, Japan, the Netherlands, Portugal, Switzerland, Turkey, the United States and Yugoslavia (all permitted, for the less-secure commercial model Enigma machines without a plugboard; and the usual arrangement was that the secret rotor wirings supplied to the customer should be disclosed to the Ministry). Even this is not the complete list, since in 1943 the firm gave the German Armed Forces High Command a list containing nine more countries to which Enigma machines had been sold. One of these was even England. A more difficult case was a Polish firm, which made contact in 1937. The company felt obliged to tell the Ministry that five commercial Enigmas had already been sold to the Polish Government in 1928; still, the sale of more commercial model Enigmas to Poland was approved in 1937.

The use of Enigma by Polish companies was of little concern, even in 1937, but perhaps the earlier sales should have set off an alarm bell. Polish military intelligence knew a lot more about Enigma than anyone in Germany would have imagined possible.

Safety in settings	
Number of combinations of rotors (choosing three from a library of five)	60
Number of ring-settings for rotors	17,576
Number of stars estimated to be in the Milky Way	between 100 and 400,000,000,000
Number of possible cross-pluggings, with ten cables	150,738,274,937,250
Total number of possible Enigma settings on a three-rotor machine with ten cross-pluggings	158,962,555,217,826,360,000

CHAPTER TWO

A new style of spying

From the first days of its rebirth at the end of World War I, Poland was under threat. The three empires which had previously partitioned Poland's territory among themselves at the end of the eighteenth century had all been defeated in the war, but the Poles were still vulnerable to the possibility of resurgence by any of those nations and their attempts to recover lost lands. The first attack came from the east, but Bolshevik Russia's incursion was fended off by the new Polish Army in 1920 with the aid of intelligence derived from codebreaking. From then on, codebreaking and national security were intimately linked in Polish strategic thinking.

German coded messages were easily intercepted in the Polish 'corridor' that separated East Prussia from the rest of the German Reich. In the mid-1920s, the interceptors and codebreakers noticed a significant change in the way messages were being disguised. You didn't need any special training to spot the difference: the new messages seemed to have their constituent letters completely randomized, whereas the old system used a 'transposition' cipher that merely mixed up the letters in the signal and transmitted them in a jumbled order. Transposition ciphers preserve the 'letter frequency' of the original language, in which **E** is the most common letter (in both English and German) and **Z** (or, in German, **Q**) the least. But when **Z** and **Q** appear just as often as **E** something different is happening. The evenness of letter distribution in the new German signals implied that the something different was highly sophisticated; in fact, it pointed to the use of machinery to carry out the encipherment. Worse, it implied the obsolescence of the favoured techniques used by codebreakers to attack substitution ciphers like those of Caesar or Vigenère.

As we have seen, the Polish authorities had got hold of a commercial model of the Enigma machine. There was every reason to suspect that the new German signals were being enciphered using something like this – something like it, but definitely not with the exact model which the Poles had in their possession. The Polish codebreakers got nowhere with it. A glimmer of hope shone briefly in January 1929, when a parcel containing an Enigma machine, which the German authorities were desperate to have delivered to them unopened, was intercepted in Warsaw. The Poles noted the German anxiety and responded by swiftly unpicking the parcel and dismantling the machine. Alas, it was another commercial model Enigma, which they quickly screwed back together and re-wrapped. They were no closer to the solution, which depended in the first instance on finding out the secret wiring scheme of the military model of Enigma which the Germans had adapted and then adopted.

To tackle the new species of cipher it was decided to recruit a new species of codebreaker. The mathematics professor at the University of Poznań was asked to talent-spot among his undergraduates – the majority of whom, having grown up in the pre-independence 'German partition' of Poland, were bilingual as well as talented mathematicians. The selected students were invited to attend an after-hours course in codes and ciphers, at the end of which there was a test; three mathematicians who excelled in the test were then invited to take up civilian jobs with the Cipher Bureau of Polish Military Intelligence. Two of them, Jerzy Różycki and Henryk Zygalski, did so immediately; the third, Marian Rejewski, did so after a year's postgraduate study at the University of Göttingen in Germany.

Marian Rejewski

Marian Rejewski was born on 16 August 1905 in the town now called Bydgoszcz. In 1905, Poland was still divided between the three occupying empires of Russia, Austria and Germany; Bydgoszcz was in the German division and therefore called 'Bromberg'. Rejewski grew up speaking German as well as Polish, an excellent background for a codebreaker. After Poland regained independence in 1918, Rejewski entered the University of Poznań as an undergraduate student in mathematics, achieving his master's degree in 1929. That year he was chosen for the special cryptology course; his stellar performance ensured he would be recruited by Polish Military Intelligence for their Cipher Office.

In 1932 the Cipher Office outpost at Poznań relocated to Warsaw, where Rejewski began work on the Enigma problem, leading first to his solution of the wiring problem with the machine itself, and then to the techniques and machines invented by the Polish codebreakers to find the settings used by the Germans to create the daily 'key'. During these remaining pre-war years Rejewski married his teenage-years sweetheart Irena Lewandowska, and two children were born, in 1934 and 1939.

On the outbreak of war, the family was left behind as Cipher Office staff were evacuated in the face of the overwhelming invasions by Germany and the USSR. A chaotic few weeks resulted in the codebreakers regrouping under Gustave Bertrand in France. Curiously, and notwithstanding the German invasion of France in the spring of 1940, the Polish codebreakers continued to work under Bertrand secretly in the unoccupied south of the country until late 1942, when the Germans completed their occupation of the country. Rejewski, together with Henryk Zygalski, managed to escape over the mountains to Spain, only to be arrested by the Spanish police and interned until the end of July 1943. Then they were able to get away to Britain and continue their codebreaking operations under the auspices of the Polish General Staff in exile.

Marian Rejewski.

After the war, Rejewski returned to Poland and to his family, but spent the first few years under suspicion and investigation because of his very obscure war record which the Communist authorities found disturbing. By the mid-1950s the investigations lapsed, though the accountancy jobs Rejewski was given hardly reflected his genius. In 1967, though, he wrote a short memoir of his experiences in the Cypher Office, which was deposited in the Warsaw Military Historical Institute. This was discovered by the Polish historian Władysław Kozaczuk, leading eventually to the recognition of Rejewski's astonishing achievement and, today, to his status as a Polish national hero. Rejewski died aged 74 in 1980, having been awarded a clutch of medals and honours to celebrate his work.

For some reason the three mathematicians were not put to work directly on the Enigma problem. That only changed in December 1931, when their boss, Lieutenant Colonel Gwido Langer, received an early Christmas gift. His Santa Claus was a young French officer called Gustave Bertrand, who had a rather remarkable tale to tell – a tale of old-fashioned spying and skulduggery.

For Bertrand, the story began a few weeks earlier, when he was asked by one of his colleagues in the French Intelligence Service to come to a secret rendezvous to check out some code books. Buying and selling code books was Bertrand's *métier*, so he was the right man for the job. The code books were being offered for sale by a walk-in agent; walk-ins are not always reliable, especially when they are on the lookout for cash, so it was important to have an expert to assess the goods before money changed hands. Bertrand adopted the pseudonym 'Barsac' and went to meet the agent, along with his Franco-German minder, in a Belgian hotel, on 7 November 1931.

The agent was called Herr Schmidt, a name so ordinary that it needed no disguise. But Schmidt's job was in the holy of holies, the Cipher Agency of the German Defence Ministry, where his older brother was the head of the agency. This older brother, Rudolf, had not only given the younger brother, Hans-Thilo, a job but also a key to the safe where the secrets were stored. Hans-Thilo needed cash,

Gustave Bertrand, the French military intelligence officer who led the early efforts to unlock Engima's secrets.

rather a lot of it, to fund a lifestyle which a civil service salary would not permit, and the temptation of the safe and its contents was too great to resist. So, Hans-Thilo had walked into the French Embassy in Berlin and asked to speak to the Military Attaché. Spying in the old-fashioned way meant cover-names for agents, so Schmidt became Agent 'Asche' (in German) or 'H.E.' (in French, which is pronounced the same way). It also meant setting up meetings in a roundabout and clandestine fashion, with obscurely-worded postcards sent to anonymous PO boxes. And it meant that Schmidt, or Asche, had to sneak the documents out of the safe late on a Friday, and be able to put them back unobserved before the office re-opened the following Monday. It was terrifying, exhilarating, and it was about to be richly rewarding.

Gustave Bertrand looked at the documents in the quiet of the upstairs bathroom of the hotel, where he could lock himself in with a camera and not draw attention to himself. Meanwhile, Schmidt and the minder sat in the bar and drank whisky and smoked cigars. What Bertrand had been offered was not just genuine stuff but pure gold: it was the operating instructions, and key-setting methodology, of the German Army's special-model Enigma machine. Nothing like this had leaked out of German hands before. It was worth every pfennig of the 5,000 Reichsmarks which Schmidt received – around a whole year's salary for a single weekend's treachery.

Back in Paris the photographs of the documents snaffled from the safe were rapidly developed and delivered up to Bertrand's colleagues in the French Cipher Section. The cipher experts were dismissive. Operating instructions and key-setting procedures were no use whatever without knowing the wiring pattern which the Germans had adopted for their military version of the Enigma machine. Bertrand thought this brush-off told him more about the capabilities of his colleagues than the worth of his documents, so he decided to reach

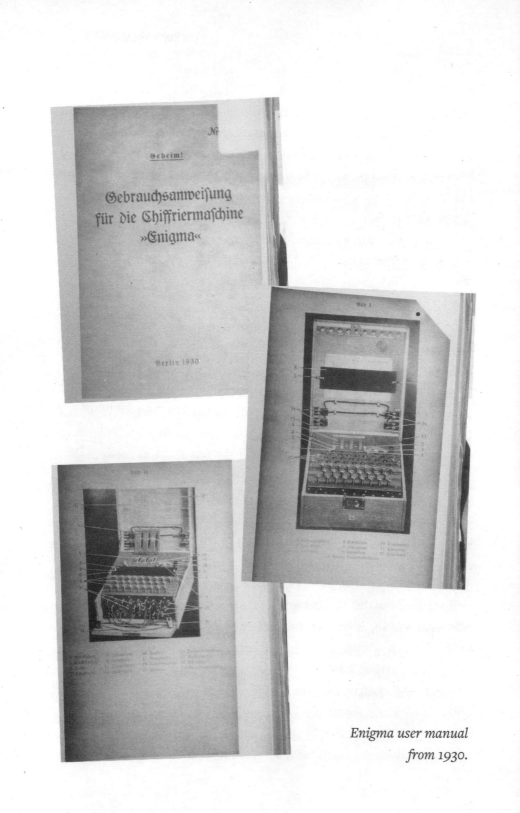

Enigma user manual from 1930.

out to France's allies: first of all, the British – who gave him much the same answer as the French Cipher Section – and then the Poles, with whom France had had a military intelligence partnership since the end of World War I. The reaction Bertrand received from Langer, after making the long train journey from Paris to Warsaw with his Christmas parcel, was quite different. Langer told Bertrand that the photographs were 'heavy artillery' – the big guns which could blow up the Enigma secret once and for all. Bertrand was delighted; and Langer promised to let him know if the Polish codebreakers got anywhere with what they had just been given.

For reasons which have since become obscured, it took until the autumn of 1932 before Langer put Marian Rejewski to work on the problem of Enigma. The available material was rather limited: Bertrand's photographs, of course; the commercial model Enigma in the Polish Army's possession, with the wrong wirings and no plugboard; some intercepted messages; and some monthly key-sheets supplied by Hans-Thilo Schmidt at a later handover meeting in mid-1932. Nevertheless, Rejewski soon figured out that the problem of the unknown wirings was a problem in permutation theory – exactly the subject matter of one of the courses he had attended at university in Poznań.

With the help of the pictures showing the main features of the German Army Enigma machine, Rejewski reasoned that each of its components was responsible for a substitution of all 26 letters of the alphabet: the plugboard, the QWERTZU wiring connecting plugboard and entry-plate, the three moving rotors and the turnaround wheel: he named them S, E, C_1, C_2, C_3 and U respectively.

The first breakthrough achieved by Marian Rejewski was by exploiting the 'message setting' information contained in the opening sequence of letters of each enciphered message. This told the receiver how to orientate the three rotors in his machine. The procedure was

Hans-Thilo Schmidt – an enigma of spying

Hans-Thilo Schmidt was born on 18 May 1893. We know little about his background except that – despite the very ordinary surname – on his mother's side there was some link to minor German aristocracy. Schmidt's elder brother Rudolf was a professional soldier, and both brothers served in World War I – where Hans-Thilo was awarded an Iron Cross. After the war, things went less well for him, though Rudolf maintained a staff role in the severely diminished German Army. Hans-Thilo, by contrast, is said to have led a less upright lifestyle, with serial seductions of his children's nannies and aspirations to a playboy lifestyle.

Hans-Thilo's fame rests entirely on his star turn as a spy for the French. While nowadays he is best known for filching the Enigma documents from the safe in his brother's office in 1931, he was considered by French intelligence to be their greatest asset. In addition to more than 300 documents relating to codes and ciphers, he handed over a huge range of vital secrets. The most productive years for the French came after 1934, when Schmidt came into a role which granted him access to one of the most secret spying organizations at the nerve-centre of the Nazis' peculiar structure. This was the *Forschungsamt* – the 'Research Office', a name which gave nothing away, but was the intelligence service specially set up by Hermann Göring to spy for the Party. Schmidt carried on spying for the French until well after the war began. From the *Forschungsamt* Schmidt was able to get hold of papers and information of astonishing significance, for example the dates planned for the invasion of Poland, and the operational intention to cut off the British and French armies by the northward 'sickle-cut' drive that led to the Dunkirk evacuation.

Eventually, the truth caught up with him. In 1943 his handler was arrested in the south of France and gave away to the Germans the identity of his source. Schmidt was in turn arrested, and took his own life later that year while in custody. Meanwhile his brother Rudolf, who had become a successful tank general, was relieved of his command.

that the sender would encipher, twice over, the starting-position (message setting) on the Enigma machine itself. This gave a sequence of six letters which showed, albeit in hidden form, how the progression of the fast rotor would change the encipherment.

Rejewski also figured out that while this sequence was being enciphered it was likely that the middle and slow rotors of the machine would be stationary. This meant that C_2, C_3 and U could be collapsed into a single unknown which didn't change, unlike C_1, while the rest of the sequence was enciphered. Rejewski was therefore able to create six equations – one for each of the six letters of the preamble containing the message setting. But he still had too many unknowns for a solution of the equations to be within reach. One of them was the plugboard settings, but he'd been given those for the last two quarters of 1932 in a new package of materials supplied via Bertrand by Hans-Thilo Schmidt. There were still three to go: the QWERTZU, the fast rotor C_1, and the compound substitution of the other rotors and turnaround wheel. Normally, with six equations and only three unknowns, the unknowns should be easy to find. But permanent equations are very difficult to solve, and Rejewski reckoned that in this case the solution would be impossible.

Then Rejewski had an inspiration, about the QWERTZU. The QWERTZU wiring pattern was different from the commercial model, where the connections were in alphabetical order: **Q** wired to **A**, **W** to **B**, **E** to **C**, and so on. But maybe the wires connecting the plugboard and the entry plate in the military machine was simpler still: perhaps **A** was wired to **A**, **B** to **B**, and so on. He tried it. Fewer unknowns would bring the equations within reach. It was inspired, and it worked. The substitution structures of C_1 and the compounded remaining rotors came out; the next month, October 1932, for which he had keys, involved a different rotor in the fast position, giving a new C_1, and then the remaining unknowns, U and the last rotor, could fairly simply be worked out.

The mathematical approach – reducing the wiring problem to equations which could, with a great deal of effort and trial-and-error, be solved – meant that Rejewski was able, by the beginning of 1933, to describe to engineers in the Cipher Bureau how the German military Enigma machine was wired up. The engineers, led by Antoni Palluth – who happened to be the first officer anywhere to have made an attempt on the Enigma problem – were able to reconstruct a fully functioning Enigma machine. It wasn't an Enigma, because the plugboard was at the back and the keyboard was arranged in alphabetical rather than German QWERTZU order, but that didn't matter. It did the job.

Still, as the Germans had already realized, having a machine was only half the battle. Because they had foreseen the possibility of battlefield captures of the physical equipment, the security of Enigma was principally achieved through the secrecy of the 'key', or the way the machine was set up every day. It wasn't wise to rely on Christmas gifts from Hans-Thilo Schmidt to provide a supply of the key-sheets: the Polish codebreakers needed to invent a new form of spying. They needed to be able to find out the key through cryptanalysis – from nothing more than the content of the enciphered messages themselves.

With some help from the documents stolen by Schmidt, Rejewski had already deconstructed the opening sequence of letters in every message. These days we would refer to this sequence as metadata, or 'envelope information', since they told the recipient of the message how to set the three rotors in the Enigma machine for decryption. All the other information was given in key-sheets, and would have to be rebuilt by the codebreakers; but Rejewski had spotted that the message-setting metadata gave away clues about the order in which the rotors had been put into the machine. The clues came from the way that the information about the rotor orientation was conveyed. Basically, the sender had to tell the receiver which number should show

Polish reverse-engineered Enigma equivalent.

through the small viewing window in the metal cover of the Enigma machine – for each rotor, which of the 26 possible orientations chosen was dictated by the number, 01 to 26, visible through the window. The sender could have set the rotors to 07, 14, 23 and composed his message with the corresponding letters **G, N, W** as the metadata, but that would be something of a giveaway, so the procedure was to encipher the setting **GNW** – using the Enigma machine itself. In the earliest days the 'ground-setting' for enciphering the three-letter signal **GNW** (or whatever the operator chose) was provided as part of the key-sheet; by the time World War II began, operators chose a ground-setting for themselves and added the chosen setting onto the start of the metadata.

So far, then, the sender was going to encipher **GNW** using some ground-setting unknown to Mr Rejewski and his colleagues in the Polish Cipher Bureau. But German procedure up to May 1940 was to encipher these three letters twice over, in case of garbles or difficult radio conditions: a single false letter could render the entirety of the message unreadable. So, the sender set his machine to the unknown ground-setting prescribed by his key-sheet, and typed in **GNW** twice over. Usually, this led to a seemingly random sequence like **DRKJYO**; that sequence formed the first six letters of the transmitted signal. Then the operator re-set his rotors to 07, 14, 23, as planned, and began enciphering the substantive message. The receiver would decipher **DRKJYO** using the ground-setting prescribed by the key-sheet, getting **GNWGNW**, and could set his rotors to 07, 14, 23 to recover the rest of the message. Excellent stuff, but Rejewski found patterns in these apparently random opening sequences.

Occasionally there were repeats in the six-letter opening sequence: things like **HJEDJQ** or **PVFPNA**: the same letter typed by the sender on his machine had enciphered in the same way in two different places in the sequence. In these examples, the same (albeit unknown) letter in the twice-enciphered metadata had yielded the same letter (**J** in the first example, **P** in the second). Rejewski soon realized that these occasional repeats were characteristic of the choice of rotor-order in the machine, and could provide a way of discovering the remaining unknown features of the key.

At about this stage in Rejewski's researches, his former colleagues from the Poznań mathematics course Jerzy Różycki and Henryk Zygalski were brought in on the Enigma project, and key-recovery research really took off. The 'characteristic' observed by Rejewski was a very powerful tool, because some rotor arrangements gave rise to many more of the opening-sequence repeats than others. The team invented a machine called the cyclometer which facilitated the analysis of these characteristics, so the codebreakers could compile a catalogue of potential repeats and make an informed guess at the rotor order.

The Polish codebreakers had now enough of an edge to be able to tease out the key – the way the German Enigmas were set up for encipherment – and to configure their own fake Enigma machines to read the German signals for themselves. Without a gap, from early 1933 the Polish intelligence service was informed in real time of the content of secret German signals enciphered on the safest machine cipher system yet invented: new-style spying had come into its own. But spying is something that has to be kept secret, so the Polish Cipher Bureau revealed nothing about its own secret success. Even Gustave Bertrand, who made periodic visits to see his friends in Poland, usually bringing some goodies from Agent Asche's latest safe-raid, was told nothing.

The Poles could not yet bask in the glories of their achievement. Codemaking and codebreaking are a game of cat and mouse, with the codemakers constantly changing their procedures and systems to foil any attempt to break their security. Any process that continues

The Polish cryptologists Marian Rejewski
(top left), Jerzy Różycki (top right)
and Henryk Zygalski (bottom).

unchanged for too long allows a body of evidence to build up, and that would give the centuries-old codebreaking techniques a chance of success. So:

- In February 1936, rotor order and cross-pluggings were changed monthly – previously the same set-up had been in effect for three months at a time.
- In October 1936, the rotor order and cross-pluggings were changed daily, and the number of cross-pluggings to be used was also changed.
- In November 1937, a new turnaround wheel was brought into operation.
- In September 1938, the centrally-mandated ground-setting – the rotor orientations used to encipher the message metadata applicable to a whole day's traffic – was discontinued in favour of user-chosen ground-settings which varied from one message to another.
- In December 1938, two new rotors were made available, making it necessary to choose three rotors from the collection afresh every day, as well as the left-to-right order in which the chosen rotors were to go into the machine.

It was no coincidence that these changes came along as the tempo of German rearmament increased, and more military Enigma traffic was detectable in the airwaves. But the Polish codebreakers were just about able to keep pace. Their machine techniques became ever more sophisticated. The change made by the Germans in September 1938 prompted a fresh round of invention, with a new variety of machine to find rotor settings of intercepted messages containing repeats in their starting sequence. These devices were named the 'bomba' machines. By automating the search for settings the much greater variety of settings now being used was only a complication, not a problem. The bomba could search through all possible positions of three rotors – 26 × 26 × 26, or 17,576 positions – in just over an hour and a half, stopping its run when it thought it had a setting which could generate three sets of duplicated letters in Enigma message preambles.

The real problem which looked set to defeat even bomba technology came along in December 1938 with the extra rotors. It wasn't particularly hard for the Polish team to recover the wiring pattern for the new rotors, but the challenge was that they no longer had enough bomba machines for the variety of rotor orders. It was a simple problem of scale in mathematics, and it looked set to defeat the Poles just at the moment when Hitler's aggressive noise reached a crescendo. With three rotors, there are only six options for the operator when putting them into the Enigma machine: **I, II, III; I, III, II; II, I, III; II, III, I; III, I, II;** and **III, II, I**. With five rotors the number of options is 60. But the Poles needed one bomba for each possibility, so they had only six of these machines; now they needed, immediately, 54 more. The success rate in reading Enigma-enciphered messages fell to 10 per cent of its previous level. The problem looked insuperable. Maybe it was time to reach out to others for help.

The Polish bomba

The logic of the Polish *bomba kryptologyczna* depended on the German procedure – abandoned in May 1940 – of repeating part of the preamble to enciphered messages.

The preamble consisted of two parts: (1) the 'ground-setting', transmitted without any disguise, telling the receiver how to orientate the three Enigma rotors to decipher the next part of the message; and (2) the 'message setting', enciphered *twice over* using the ground-setting. Thus, a preamble would look something like **KOQ RGNWWY**.

Marian Rejewski had observed that some preambles had repeated letters in the six-letter message-setting component, corresponding to the same letter in the pre-encipherment message setting. These were called 'females', and the function of the bomba was to find the actual rotor orientation by analysing females.

The bomba had six stacks of rotors which behaved like the inner parts of six Enigma machines. These would all rotate so as to test, in sequence, every one of the 17,576 possible rotor orientations. Let us imagine that the Poles had found messages which had the following preambles, each of which has females:

WTK NJZNMR   REV BLJXLS   OQA VFZUGZ

We can see that some (as yet unknown) letter in the actual message setting gave **N** in positions 1 and 4 of the enciphered message setting when the rotors began at **WTK**, some (other, unknown) letter gave **L** in positions 2 and 5 with the rotors set at **REV**, and a third unknown letter gave **Z** in positions 3 and 6 with the rotors beginning at **OQA**. The principle was to search for a single rotor orientation which could allow all these things to happen.

Each pair of rotor-stacks on the bomba was initially set to one of the ground-settings, **WTK**, **REV** or **OQA**. These were then offset to reflect the position of the observed female: by 1 and 4 in the case of the **WTK** stacks, by 2 and 5 for the **REV** stacks, and by 3 and 6 for the **OQA** stacks. Then each pair was linked to its test letter – the observed female – **N** in the case of the **WTK** stacks, **L** for the **REV** stacks, and **Z** for the **OQA** stacks. The test letter was selected for each pair of stacks by throwing a switch on one of three columns of switches on the front of the machine. Then it was set to go; and it would stop when it had found a possible position which logically permitted females to appear in the observed places.

The Polish Bomba machine.

Although it has been possible to reconstruct the principle of operation of the bomba, unfortunately no detailed diagrams or engineering descriptions of the machine have survived. So we still do not know how the logical system of the machine was brought to reality, how the stopping mechanism worked, or how the stacks of rotors achieved functional equivalence to the dual passage of current through the three rotors and turnaround wheel of a real Enigma machine. What we do know is that the principle of automated testing was a powerful influence on the design of the Bletchley Park Bombe which came into its own when the Germans desisted from double-encipherment of the message-setting component of preambles.

Breaking machines with a pencil

Far away from Warsaw, the British had not been ignoring the Enigma machine. They counted themselves among the several countries which had looked at the early offerings of Arthur Scherbius to see if they might be suitable for secret diplomatic or military communications. There were demonstrations of an early model of an Enigma machine at the Treasury in January 1926, and at the Foreign Office, with Admiralty and War Office officials present, in March 1926. Things bumbled along for a while, with Commander Edward Travis of the Government Code & Cypher School (GC&CS) – the agency established after World War I to break codes and advise on security of coded signals – planning to go to Berlin to check the newest version of the device for himself and report back to the British government's Cypher Machines Committee, for which he acted as an advisor. His visit didn't take place until 1928, after the Admiralty had expressed a positive interest in getting the machine for itself. The Admiralty's interest was sparked in 1928, after the British had digested intelligence that the German armed forces had themselves decided to adopt the machine.

In April 1928 the Cypher Machines Committee described Enigma as 'a good foreign machine.' The Committee also noted:

> Enigma – It was very doubtful whether foreign machines could ever be taken up but occasionally purchase might be desirable in order to keep in touch with developments of this type of machine. The Admiralty is contemplating the purchase of 2 sample machines and has placed a preliminary order.

It seems that Travis acquired a machine and brought it back to London. It was one of the simpler versions, with a moveable turnaround wheel but no plugboard, and it was handed over to Hugh Foss. Foss was dauntingly clever and looked the part of the wild eccentric, being 1.96m tall (6ft 5in) and adorned with a long red beard. Later in his career he would master the Japanese codes and become head of Bletchley Park's Japanese section. But in 1928 his task was to check out the security of the Germans' new-fangled machine cryptography.

For his attack, Hugh Foss realized rather quickly that the regular mileage-meter movement of the Enigma rotors was a great help to him – its predictability eliminated vast numbers of the annoying cipher permutations which Scherbius's marketing material had trumpeted. The left-most rotor was most unlikely to move during the encipherment of a short piece of text, and even the middle rotor would move only once every 26 letters. So, most of the time, it was safe to assume that there was only one moving rotor, the one on the right. That meant that the rest of the machine – the two moving rotors, and the turnaround wheel – could be assumed to be a static 'lump' which just carried out a single letter-for-letter substitution.

The British buy an Enigma machine

During the 1920s the British Government set up a Committee to think about 'Cypher Machines'. Chaired by the Treasury, it brought in interested personnel from military and civil departments, and relied heavily on the expertise of Edward Travis, a senior figure from the Government Code & Cypher School (who, during World War II, was destined to become its head).

Among various devices put forward as possible candidates for mechanical encipherment of secret British messages was the Enigma machine. Travis engaged in on-off negotiations, via the British Embassy in Berlin, to obtain such a machine. A machine was indeed acquired. Still, four years later, the position over cipher machines was that the Admiralty had decided they 'definitely do not require one'; the War Office and Air Ministry were 'anxious to obtain something quicker than present methods'; and the civil departments were still wondering how to continue to communicate with the Empire if cables were cut in a war. Enigma was not – or not exactly – destined to be the solution for the cipher security of the British Empire.

He then created a series of charts, one for each of the three rotors which could be used in the right-most position, showing what transformation the rotor carried out, whichever letter of the alphabet was keyed in and whichever orientation the rotor was in. Once they were spelt out, the series of charts provided a 'useful aspect from the point of view of a solver.'

Then he could fall back on one of the traditional tools of cipher-breakers: the technique of the 'probable word'. If you knew, or could guess at, the likely content of the enciphered message, then you had a big clue about how the cipher – or the two unknown features of the Enigma machine – transformed plain text into random burble. A sad feature of humans and their languages is that there is a high degree of predictability and redundancy in communication: junior officers and diplomats must address their generals and ministers with due respect, and so phrases like 'I beg the honour to report' are the cryptanalytic equivalent of leaving a window unlocked to enable burglars to gain entry to juicier contents beyond. And the reciprocal machine provided a handy hint at where a 'probable word' (or, as the British called it, a 'crib') might be a good fit: the inability of the machine to encipher a letter as itself. So 'honour' could not fit if an **H** was found in the first letter-position, or an **O** in the second, or so on. By treating the non-moving group of rotors and the turnaround wheel as a static assembly, he was able to devise a test for which rotor was in the right-most position. It would need a lot of trial and error, and might be tedious, but it wouldn't take forever.

Foss's report set out a detailed methodology for would-be code-breakers encountering this type of Enigma machine, together with worked examples. He illustrated his methods with paper versions of Enigma machines, with slideable paper strips representing the rotors and showing how the interior wiring switched the letters around. Foss could break Enigma encipherment with nothing more sophisticated than a pencil and squared paper.

'It will be seen from these remarks that the weak points of the Reciprocal Enigma are (1) The fact that the order of the letters against the wheels (ie QWERTZU etc) is not easily changed. (2) The principle of the counter on which the wheels are turned,' he wrote. Foss's insights were profound. His principle number (1) was exactly what the German armed forces had perceived, and to add flexibility to the input of the electricity to the rotors they had added a plugboard between the keyboard and the entry-plate. For the main armed forces this was the development which constituted the main improvement in Enigma's security. As to Foss's principle number (2), the answer was to randomize the turnover points on the rotors, so they rotated with a less uniform, predictable movement. The German armed forces did not generally adopt this until late in the war.

Foss's handwritten report wasn't typed up. By providing the cryptanalytic method alongside the description of the machine, Foss had shown that Enigma messages weren't going to be secure from foreign prying eyes. The British were not going to adopt an insecure machine: and by the time the British became seriously interested in Enigma again, it was because Germany was once again expected to be a hostile power, and the British wanted to understand the secrets of Enigma from the viewpoint of cryptanalysts rather than potential adopters of new technology. By then, the German armed forces had (without the benefit of seeing Mr Foss's report) added a plugboard, as per recommendation (1).

For a long time, Britain had not worried about Germany. In the 1920s Bolshevik Russia posed a more overt threat, and cryptanalytic effort was directed that way for many years. This may explain why the British brushed off the French approach in 1932, when Gustave Bertrand offered the documents spirited out of the Berlin safe by Hans-Thilo Schmidt; but it certainly meant that the German military adaptation of the Enigma machine was something that came and went without much study.

Foss's theory of an attack on Enigma

Although it was not feasible to work out the manifold electrical routings that the 'lump' of unmoving rotors could give rise to, it was possible to use its immobility to devise a consistency test to identify the right-hand rotor and its initial setting. Foss constructed tables, one for each rotor which could be used in the right-hand position, showing what transformation would occur through the effect of that rotor alone. Electricity could reach that rotor at any one of its 26 contacts, depending on what was keyed on the keyboard, and the rotor itself could be in any one of 26 positions, giving a table of 26 × 26 possible transformations. Each row in Foss's tables corresponded to a contact point reached on the assembly of unmoving rotors, reached via the transformation effected by the right-hand rotor.

Hugh Foss's conception of static and moving parts in an Enigma machine

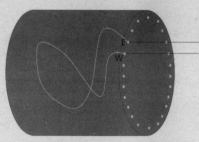
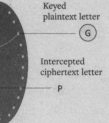

Keyed
plaintext letter

(G)

Intercepted
ciphertext letter

P

Fixed transformation made by static assembly
of two rotors and turnaround wheel

Transformation made by left-hand
rotor at position 1

Now Foss could apply a consistency test to see which rotor was in the right-hand position. If a crib suggested that the word **GENERAL** had become enciphered as **POYWZBW**, the text could be followed, through his tables, as if it were electricity flowing virtually through an actual Enigma machine.

Let's assume that the right-hand rotor is number **I** and has the number **26** showing through the viewing window on the Enigma machine. When the operator presses down the letter **G** on the Enigma machine, the rotor moves on one step (now showing number 1 in the window), and the contact on the notional assembly of unmoving rotors which becomes live is the one which sits adjacent to the counterpart to **G** as transformed by the right-hand rotor; Foss's table for rotor I indicates that that is contact **E** on the assembly. Foss's table also indicates that the letter **P** found in the ciphertext results from the contact **W** on the assembly having become live, with the right-hand rotor in position 1. That means that the assembly always converts **E** to **W**. At the next keystroke, the rotor moves to position 2, the right-hand rotor turns the letter **E** of **GENERAL** into **H** and reaches the letter **O** in our observed ciphertext from contact **Q**, telling us that the assembly converts **H** to **Q**. The process can be continued throughout the rest of the word **GENERAL/POYWZBW**.

An inconsistency will show up if the table indicated that contact point **E** was connected via the assembly of unmoving rotors to **W** at one place in the encoded message but **L** at another. This wouldn't be logically allowed, since electricity can only follow a single path through the static assembly – so the choice of starting-point for the encryption must be wrong and a different starting-point should be used. (There were, of course, other reasons why an inconsistency could show up: for example, there might be a turnover of the middle rotor, defeating the principle of a static assembly of all rotors apart from the right-hand one; a different rotor might be in the right-hand position; or the crib might just be a bad guess.)

Britain's next brush with Enigma came with the outbreak of the Spanish Civil War in 1936. Franco and his Nationalist insurgency were supported by fellow-fascist Mussolini; and both of them were using a version of the 'Model K Enigma', supplied by their allies in Germany. Model K Enigma machines had three moving rotors, a turnaround wheel which could be set into any one of 26 positions, and no plugboard. In fact, they were almost exactly the same thing as that which Foss had analysed a few years before, albeit with different rotors. This time, though, the attack on Enigma was being done not by Foss, but by Dilly Knox.

Alfred Dillwyn Knox was one of the greatest codebreakers. In World War I he had been part of the famous 'Room 40' team in the Admiralty which not only figured out through cryptanalysis where German ships were deployed but also broke the 'Zimmermann Telegram', a top-secret message from Germany's foreign minister which tried to tempt Mexico to join forces with Germany and Austria-Hungary in that conflict. The scheme backfired because the quid pro quo offered to Mexico was the return of various states, by then part of the USA, which had become American after the previous century's Mexican war. Britain leaked the contents of the telegram to the US authorities, outrage followed, and the result was that the United States entered the war on the Franco-British side, rather than Mexico on the Austro-German one. Even in his spare time, as a fellow of King's College, Cambridge, Knox was a genius at piecing together coded material – his work piecing together fragments of text by the Greek poet Herodas was, in effect, an exercise in codebreaking as much as one in solving a jigsaw puzzle.

Knox took up the Enigma problem where Foss had left off seven years before, recovering the new rotor wiring through exploitation of the reciprocal Enigma's famous weakness: that no letter could encipher as itself. He then set about devising a codebreaking method using 'rods' – short cardboard sticks on which the substitution effect of the right-hand rotor was recorded, for each of the 26 electrical contacts on its right-hand face. This was an adaptation from Foss's charts, but the little rods could also be used to recover missing parts of the plaintext where unknown enciphered letters in the intercepted message, outside the crib sequence, also appeared in other places on the rods. By applying codebreakers' traditional linguistic methods of guessing at blanks in between known letters – rather like filling in a crossword puzzle – more of the picture could be coloured in, and further deductions using additional rods could be made. Sooner or later, without having to know the mysteries going on in the 'static' part of the machine, enough information might appear not only to disclose the remainder of the message but also to figure out the possible set-up of the machine.

The principle behind 'rodding' is that the rods identify the contact on the middle rotor which is reached when a letter is pressed on an Enigma machine which has no plugboard. A rod is created for each one of the 26 possible contacts. Taking one of those contacts, say contact **Q**, the **Q**-contact rod is divided into 26 further sections, one for each position of the right-hand rotor. What the rod lists is the keyboard letter which must be pressed in each of those positions to enable the **Q**-contact on the middle rotor to be reached. A rod might therefore look something like this (to keep it simple only a few squares are shown):

	1	2	3	4	5	6	7	8	9	10	11	12	13	14
Q	C	U	L	H	I	V	Y	R	P	S	D	M	T	K

Now the codebreaker looks at the intercepted ciphertext and guesses that it might be an encipherment of a particular crib, such as the word **GEHEIM** ('secret'). The ciphertext had the letter **J** in the fifth place in the message, implying that the Enigma machine turned **I** into **J** at that point. The codebreaker then chooses a pair of rods which have letters **I** or **J** in position 6, thus:

	1	2	3	4	5	6	7	8	9	10	11	12	13	14
Q	C	U	L	H	I	V	Y	R	P	S	D	M	T	K
Z	Q	N	O	B	J	K	R	A	V	U	Y	W	C	W

This pair implies that the static pair of rotors and the turnaround wheel connected the **Q**-contact and the **Z**-contact on the middle rotor.

Other pairs of rods can be picked to reflect other encryptions of the crib. So long as there is no inconsistency with the implied contacts on the middle rotor, the pairs can be kept (clearly if **Q** is electrically connected to **Z**, **Q** could not be connected to some other letter like **K** instead).

Now, it might be possible to read off other letters found in the ciphertext. If, say, the thirteenth letter of the ciphertext was **C**, then the rod-pair suggests that its plaintext counterpart was **T**, because in position 13 electricity enters the middle rotor at the **Q**-contact (again) if the letter **T** is pressed on the Enigma keyboard, and emerges at the **Z**-contact (again), this time yielding **C** once the current passes through the right-hand rotor.

By building up some of the letters from the message, it can be possible to interpolate more words of the plaintext, thereby extending the crib, and bringing more rod-pairs into play. Eventually the sense of the message may emerge.

Knox was reportedly so excited by his breakthrough on Enigma that he rediscovered the energy and enthusiasm which he had first experienced during World War I. But this came at a price – he was so worried that he might inadvertently let slip some frightful secret that, for the first time ever, Knox declined the invitation from King's College, Cambridge, to their annual founder's feast.

	1	2	3	4	5	6	7	8	9	10	11	12	13	14	15	16	17	18	19	20	21	22	23	24	25	26
Q	12	15	5	16	22	8	2	20	23	6	7	26	10	11	4	17	9	11	3	1	20	14	7	13	6	24
W	16	6	17	23	9	3	21	24	7	8	1	11	12	5	18	10	12	4	2	21	15	8	14	7	25	13
E	7	18	24	10	4	22	25	8	9	2	12	13	6	19	11	13	5	3	22	16	9	15	8	26	14	17
R	19	25	11	5	23	26	9	10	3	13	14	7	20	12	14	6	4	23	17	10	16	9	1	15	18	8
T	26	12	6	24	1	10	11	4	14	15	8	21	13	15	7	5	24	18	11	17	19	2	16	19	9	20
Z	13	7	25	2	11	12	5	15	16	9	22	14	16	8	6	25	19	12	18	11	3	17	20	10	21	1
U	8	26	3	12	13	6	16	17	10	23	15	17	9	7	26	20	13	19	12	9	18	21	11	22	2	14
I	1	4	13	14	7	17	18	11	24	16	18	10	8	1	21	14	20	13	5	19	22	12	23	6	15	9
O	5	14	15	8	18	19	12	25	17	19	11	9	2	22	15	24	14	6	20	23	13	24	4	16	10	2
A	15	16	9	19	20	13	26	18	20	12	10	3	23	16	22	15	7	21	24	14	25	5	17	11	3	6
S	17	10	20	21	14	1	19	21	13	11	4	24	17	23	16	8	22	25	15	26	6	18	12	4	7	16
D	11	21	22	15	2	20	22	14	12	5	25	18	24	17	9	23	26	16	1	7	19	13	5	8	17	18
F	22	23	16	3	21	23	15	13	6	26	19	25	18	10	24	1	17	2	8	20	14	6	9	18	19	12
G	24	17	4	22	24	16	14	7	1	20	26	19	4	25	2	18	3	9	21	15	7	10	19	20	13	23
H	18	5	23	25	17	15	8	2	21	1	20	12	26	3	19	4	10	22	16	8	11	20	21	14	24	25
J	6	24	26	18	16	9	3	22	2	25	13	1	4	20	5	11	23	17	9	12	4	22	15	25	26	19
K	25	1	19	17	10	4	23	3	22	14	2	5	21	6	12	24	18	10	13	22	23	16	26	1	20	7
P	2	20	18	11	5	24	4	23	15	3	6	22	7	13	25	19	11	14	23	24	17	1	2	24	8	26
Y	21	19	12	6	25	5	24	16	4	7	23	8	14	26	20	12	15	24	25	18	2	3	22	9	1	3
X	20	13	7	26	6	25	17	5	8	24	9	15	1	21	13	16	25	26	19	3	4	23	10	2	4	22
C	14	8	1	7	26	18	6	9	25	10	16	2	22	14	17	24	1	20	4	5	24	11	3	5	23	21
V	9	2	8	1	19	7	10	26	11	17	3	23	15	18	1	2	24	5	6	25	12	4	6	24	22	15
B	3	9	2	20	8	11	1	12	18	4	24	16	19	2	3	22	6	7	26	13	5	7	25	23	16	10
N	10	3	24	9	12	2	13	19	5	25	17	20	3	4	23	7	8	1	14	6	8	26	24	17	11	4
M	4	22	10	13	3	14	20	6	26	18	21	4	5	24	8	4	2	15	7	9	1	25	18	12	5	11
L	23	11	14	4	15	21	7	1	19	22	5	6	25	9	10	3	16	8	10	2	26	19	13	6	12	5
	1	2	3	4	5	6	7	8	9	10	11	12	13	14	15	16	17	18	19	20	21	22	23	24	25	26

Foss's chart for Rotor I.

Dilly Knox

The reputation of Dillwyn Knox (known as Dilly) was only partly built on his brilliance as a codebreaker. His thinking was best done in the bath, so a bathtub was installed in the Admiralty to accommodate his curious working style. This caused minor upsets with some female staff members, but not all – one of them would become his wife. Knox was given a commission in the Royal Navy (since naval officers of that era disliked being given intelligence by civilians), but Knox's hopelessness with uniforms, saluting and discipline all contributed to the professorial aura of brilliance.

Between the wars Knox retired into academic obscurity at King's College, Cambridge, working on a codebreaking puzzle of immense difficulty but of a non-strategic nature. A badly preserved manuscript containing the bizarre and unorthodox poetry of a minor Greek poet was in tiny fragments, which had to be reassembled using the skills of a jigsaw-puzzle solver and classical linguist.

Dilly Knox.

Knox's published translation was so odd, though, that one wonders whether the effort was worthwhile.

Dilly himself was known to be a little cantankerous as well as eccentric. The cantankerousness was exceptional rather than typical, though there were certainly times when he spoke his mind, notably at the conferences with the Polish codebreakers in 1939. At Bletchley Park, when changes were mooted of which he disapproved, Knox would resign: the files at the British National Archives abound with Knox's resignation letters. Invariably, Alastair Denniston, Knox's boss, would talk him round. The fact is that Knox's personality was principally one of charm, so his curiosities – spectacles kept in his tobacco-pouch, his appalling driving, his uncompromising nature with recruits – were all forgivable. And he was brilliant, the 'Chief Cryptographer' of GC&CS.

Denniston also knew Dilly well enough to realize that things were not right with him. A Dilly letter of November 1941 begins with the understatement, 'I am in the doctor's hands for a minor ailment.' It was the early stage of something much more serious – the cancer that would take Dilly from the world in February 1943, aged only 58. Mavis Lever visited him in hospital where, she recalled, 'his brother Evoe was by his bedside and they were roaring with laughter composing Dilly's last words.'

From a strategic viewpoint, the national interests of the United Kingdom were perhaps not greatly affected by the Spanish Civil War, so the messages Knox was breaking were not going to change the course of history. But in another sense, the war was an important development. Not only did it show that the fascists were in the ascendant, and thereby help to wake up the British to the incipient threat from Germany, but it can also be seen as a prequel to the major world-engulfing conflict which was to follow. The German armed forces were using the Spanish war to test new theories of combat – and the British were using it to test their own strength at Enigma codebreaking. In the end, it was a warm-up exercise for both sides. Germany's most effective military innovations would be revealed to the world during the Blitzkrieg; and the Spanish-Italian Enigma was the school-playground version when compared with the German military machine, with its plugboard and huge multiplicity of settings.

In September 1938, John Tiltman – one of Britain's most accomplished codebreakers, and arguably the most accomplished – wrote a memo on the German military Enigma. With the Munich crisis and Hitler's expansionism now unavoidably evident, GC&CS had finally turned its mind to German codes and ciphers. Unfortunately, the German armed forces were all using the complex plugboard version of Enigma, and the British (as revealed by Tiltman's memo) were a long way behind in the race to crack its secrets. The rotor wirings were unknown and the plugboard itself was a mystery. The biggest issue was that the wiring connecting the entry-plate to the keyboard – the QWERTZU – was different from the Model K Enigma which Knox had been working on, and there seemed to be no way to fathom out what the new wiring scheme might be. The plugboard's function was clear enough from the photographs and operating instructions, which the British dug out of their archives from the handover generously made by Gustave Bertrand back in 1932. But where the plugboard sat in the electrical layout was still far from clear. In any case, even if they had known, it wouldn't have got them very far.

The problem with the German armed forces Enigma was that without knowing the QWERTZU there was no opportunity to bring Knox's techniques of rotor-wiring discovery or rodding to bear. Worse still, even if they had, the plugboard would then disguise the transformations going on inside the rotors, so that rodding would not work in any case. In a word, the British were stumped.

Captain Tiltman's memo had a purpose – to find out from the French what they knew about the plugboard Enigma. In turn, the French – led by Gustave Bertrand, who had delivered the booty to the British and the Polish six years before – were themselves very keen to find out what progress the British had made on the Enigma problem. Not just the British: Bertrand had set up liaison networks with cryptological agencies across Europe, but the strongest of these was with the Poles. Unfortunately for Bertrand, and despite his suspicions that the Poles knew more than they were letting on, he'd been told nothing of substance, not a hint of the breakthrough which Marian Rejewski and the other mathematicians had achieved.

Bertrand's softly-softly strategy was built around the idea that the more the various teams working on Enigma talked to each other, the more likely it was that bits and pieces of information could be assembled into a full-blown attack on the machine; and the Poles might be teased into revealing a little more of what they knew. So Bertrand suggested a conference, to be attended by the Polish and British codebreaking teams as well as his own. The other teams agreed, and the conference took place in Paris in January 1939.

In many ways the conference was a flop. The Polish General Staff had not authorized any substantive disclosure; the French were disproportionately proud of their approach, which followed the British in concept but was probably slightly behind; and the British concluded that the only outcome of value was the agreement to share intercepted radio traffic, which the different countries could collect in their own specific regions. It could have been worse. Dilly Knox let his exasperation show, and his boss Alastair Denniston, head of the GC&CS, had to bring his urbane charm to bear to settle the mood of the meeting.

Nevertheless, there was one conclusion, brokered by Bertrand, which had some importance. The three participating agencies each agreed that if they made a breakthrough on the Enigma problem they'd send a telegram to the others saying something had come up, or to use the French phrase agreed upon, '*Il y a du nouveau.*' For the Polish delegates, there already was plenty of *nouveau*, but there were two problems for them, pulling in opposite directions. On the one hand, the German changes to the Enigma operating method in December 1938 represented a major setback. They had only six of their bomba machines, and they needed 60 to resume their success levels of 1938; and this problem had arisen just at the time tension was mounting in Central Europe and Poland felt under the greatest threat from Nazi expansionism. On the other hand, the Polish General Staff were not yet ready to give away secrets for free, especially to states whose internal politics and reliability as allies were far from certain.

Tensions continued to mount and the Polish codebreakers could not find a solution to the bomba shortage. But one of the mathematicians, Henryk Zygalski, hit upon a brilliant alternative to the bomba which did not require vast resources of machinery. He figured that the repeated letters in the doubly-enciphered 'indicator' sent at the start of German messages – the 'females' feature which the bomba machines were designed to exploit – could be charted on large cardboard sheets. Each sheet would represent an Enigma rotor placed in the left-most position in the machine, and that rotor would be presumed to be immobile for the encipherment of the six letters of the indicator sequence used by the German Army and air force. The behaviour of the middle rotor at each of its 26 possible positions would be reflected across the horizontal axis of the sheet, and the behaviour of the 'fast' right-hand rotor along the vertical axis. This way, each of the 26×26 possibilities for the two moving rotors would be shown by its own place on the grid. Then the cardboard could be punched with a hole for each grid-position

– which is to say, each configuration of the three rotors – where a 'female' repeat was possible. Then, Zygalski reckoned, all you'd have to do is stack up the cardboard sheets on top of each other, on a light box, aligning them to reflect the indicators which had actually been used; with enough sheets the number of holes through which light shone would diminish, eventually leaving only one or two possibilities to be tested. Zygalski's sheets could take the place of bombas in finding the starting set-up of the Enigma machine, and begin to recover the lost ground.

But even Henryk Zygalski could not hold back the tide of German aggression. Poland needed the French Army to retaliate if Poland came under attack; Poland itself might not be able to resist the might of the Wehrmacht. The state needed something to trade; and the possibility of a bargain arose. The codebreakers of Warsaw were authorized to send a telegram to Paris. It read, '*Il y a du nouveau.*' A new conference was proposed, and in the third week of July 1939 the three teams prepared to reassemble in Warsaw.

On 26 July 1939 official cars brought the foreign delegations to the top-secret codebreaking hide-out specially built for them in the woods to the south of Warsaw. The secrecy and military ceremony in which the opening meetings were clothed didn't chime well with the unconventional and hobbyist ways of the likes of Dilly Knox, who became more and more convinced that he was wasting his time. At some point during the day, the Polish codebreakers disclosed that they had uncovered the mystery of the QWERTZU. They expected the news to be received with joy; instead Knox was fuming with anger, and refused to accept that such a simple conclusion as that which Rejewski had reached – that the QWERTZU was the simplest possible configuration (**A** wired to **A**, **B** to **B** and so on) – could have been arrived at by anything other than deviousness. The Poles, concluded Knox, had stolen the secret. The scene was set for a diplomatic disaster.

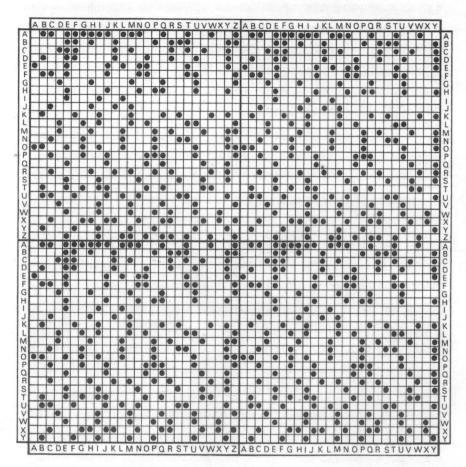

A Zygalski sheet.

Somehow – history does not tell how – Denniston coaxed Knox out of his foul temper overnight and managed to restore harmony for the second day of the conference. This time, Knox was all charm and technical brilliance, perhaps because the military bigwigs had left the day's details to the technicians like Rejewski, Różycki and Zygalski. And the lighter mood allowed more scope for revelations. The Poles revealed everything. Everything. Not just their solution of the Enigma machine's internal wiring and their methods for finding wirings of new rotors, but their own carefully crafted techniques for solving the daily set-up of the machine: the cyclometer, the Zygalski sheets, the bombas, you name it. They even promised to send across to Paris, by diplomatic bag, two copies of their reconstructed Enigma machines, one each for the French and British teams.

Only five weeks later the German tanks thrummed into Poland. The precious handover had happened just in time to save the battle against Enigma, even if it could not prevent the defeat of Poland herself.

Meanwhile, even after the war began, various powers continued to use simpler versions of Enigma which were vulnerable to traditional techniques of codebreaking. As we have seen, the Germans were careful not to distribute their strong plugboard version of the machine even to their allies, so that their Italian friends had to make do with the Model K version which Knox had mastered. This continued to be so for a year or two after World War II broke out: Italy entered the war shortly after the conflict reached Western Europe in 1940, and by then Knox and his team were on top of the problem.

Knox recruited a team of young women to assist him in this endeavour. (It's not clear why he preferred women – certainly there is no suggestion of impropriety. It's also the case that not all of his team were women, though they were definitely in the majority.) One of his recruits in 1940 was the 18-year-old Mavis Lever:

When Penelope Fitzgerald came to see me, when writing her book *The Knox Brothers*, she asked me if I could remember my actual first meeting with her uncle. I described the cottage room where he was sitting by the window in wreaths of smoke and, taking his pipe out of his mouth, he looked up and said: 'We're breaking machines. Have you got a pencil?'

Since Mavis Lever had never even heard of the Enigma machine, this must have been somewhat unsettling. In two short sentences, though, Knox had summed up the state of Enigma codebreaking at Bletchley Park in the spring of 1940. They were trying to break machines with pencils.

Still, with Italy's declaration of war a few weeks after her arrival Lever soon made her mark as a first-rate codebreaker. A standard crib for Italian naval messages was **PERX**: this was made up of the rather unimaginative idea that messages might begin with address information, thus the Italian word for 'To' and an 'X' for a space. Sometimes this worked but sometimes it didn't; Mavis noticed that the 'X' didn't fit so she tried the Italian for 'Personal' – **PERSONALE** – instead, and things fell into place. By the middle of the next year her codebreaking was so good that it was creating intelligence which was changing the war: the Battle of Matapan, a crushing defeat of the Italian Navy, was facilitated by secret intelligence derived from an Enigma message broken by Mavis Lever.

Shortly after that disaster, the Italians began to adopt different types of cipher machinery for military communications, rendering much of the work and techniques designed for Model K Enigmas obsolete. But other types of Enigma machine without plugboards were in use, and by December of 1941 a sufficient volume of signals was being sent out by the German Abwehr – their own military Intelligence Service – to be worth an assault. Knox's team was allocated the task, and they set to it with relish.

Rapidly, an analysis of Abwehr signals showed that it was a machine cipher, probably of the Enigma type: the frequency count of letters had no peaks and troughs; such randomization pointed to a machine method. Then there was an eight-letter 'indicator' opening sequence – message information suggesting that the sender was telling the receiver how to orientate four rotors, and sending the information twice over, just as the German Army had done up until May 1940. The doubly-enciphered indicator sequence was exploitable by code-breakers, as Marian Rejewski had discovered years before.

But the four-rotor Abwehr Enigma, as revealed by analysis of these opening sequences, had some very curious features. Knox named one of these features 'crabs': a 'crab' happened when all four rotors of the Enigma machine stepped on one space: something rare, one might imagine; except that all four rotors moving seemed to happen rather a lot. Specifically, a crab was a four-rotor turnover in the first four letters of the indicator sequence followed by another four-rotor turnover in the second set of four letters. Crabs weren't much use to the codebreakers beyond telling them that they were dealing with rotors with many turnover notches on them. But sometimes they found rarer sea-creatures: four-rotor turnovers occurring twice within the same sequence of four letters. These were called 'lobsters', because, according to Dilly, a lobster is half a crab; but as any fishmonger knows, lobsters are much more valuable than crabs. Using techniques similar to those of the Polish codebreakers, lobsters could be used together with guesses at the actual indicators used, to tease out more information about the Abwehr machine.

The downfall of the Abwehr Enigma was in part attributable to the German operators' tendency to choose pronounceable four-letter words for their opening sequence: words like **WEIN**, which might tell you a little of what was on the mind of German intelligence officers working in the field. Codebreakers like Knox and Lever enjoyed finding things like that, and incidentally recovering the notch patterns on the Abwehr machine rotors. One rotor, solved by Mavis Lever, had 11 notches, another 15, and a third 17. The fourth rotor doubled as a turnaround wheel, and didn't need notches because it drove no other rotors and could not be used in any other position than the left-most one.

The Abwehr machine had no plugboard, and once the machine's mechanism had been figured out, decryption could begin. Without a plugboard, and with the special attacks via lobsters, the Abwehr Enigma was susceptible to pencil-and-paper codebreaking, and began to produce some useable results. By December 1941 Knox's section was rebranded 'ISK', standing for Illicit Services Knox, since the transmissions sent by Abwehr operatives were often from places where they shouldn't actually be. ISK was to provide intelligence on the intelligence service itself: to spy on Germany's very own spies. By 1944, the information derived from ISK decrypts was to have a crucial impact on the war's direction.

By then, however, even Abwehr Enigma was being attacked with more modern technology. The volume of Abwehr traffic was small relative to other sources. Most Enigma messages – the high-volume output of the German Army, air force and navy – emanated from machines equipped with plugboards, and could never be solved through pencil-and-paper methods alone. If the content of those messages was going to be revealed within a short enough timescale to be of practical use, a quite different cryptanalytical style would have to be developed. That style would need to be automated to deal with the German assumption that safety lay in astronomically large numbers. An infusion of technological expertise was what GC&CS needed to transform Bletchley Park, to mature it from the squared-paper ethos of World War I veterans into a modern, effective business organization, thriving as much on the buzz of computing as on the brilliance of its people.

Mavis and Keith

Mavis Lever nearly didn't get to Bletchley Park. In the lead-up to the war she wanted to help refugees from Germany, and enabled a couple to find employment in a country house in Kent. The 'refugees' turned out to be spies despatched to provide intelligence for the Nazi regime, leading to an enquiry into the background of the spies' sponsor.

Mavis was cleared, and with German language and pattern-spotting skills she quickly became a codebreaker assigned to Dilly Knox's Enigma research team at the age of 19. The results, from which Matapan and the Abwehr Enigma are the stand-out achievements, were many.

One day Mavis was working on a problem which needed help from Hut 6, where the principal effort against German Army and air force Enigma was carried out. A young man called Keith Batey, a Cambridge mathematician recruited by Gordon Welchman, offered to help. He was not much older than Mavis and definitely interested, but because of the rigid compartmentalization at Bletchley the two did not meet again for another year. Keith was itching to get into active service, but knowledge of the awful Enigma secret made it difficult for him to serve in a combat zone in case he was captured.

Still, somehow, things worked out for both of them. In November 1942 Keith and Mavis were married, and within three days Keith was sent to Canada to train for the Fleet Air Arm. The wedding was attended by Margaret Rock, a distinguished codebreaker from Dilly Knox's team, and Peter Twinn, the first Bletchley mathematician and the Enigma specialist who had had to explain Alan Turing's ideas for a Bombe to the engineers at the British Tabulating Machine (BTM) company.

Keith's time in Canada came to an end when the attack on the Abwehr Enigma was prioritized and the ISK section at Bletchley needed his help. Together with Mavis, Margaret Rock and Peter Twinn, Keith led the group, with the four of them writing the official war history of ISK when peace was restored.

The post-war years saw Keith working in the diplomatic service and at the University of Oxford. In addition to becoming a writer, Mavis forged a new, unpaid, career in the conservation of historic gardens, leading to her being granted the MBE in 1988. Her role and that of Keith at Bletchley Park was in those days still almost wholly unrecognized, though by the time of their deaths in 2013 and 2010 respectively that had changed.

Mavis and Keith have an enduring, if somewhat unlikely, memorial in the Hollywood film *Enigma* starring Dougray Scott and Kate Winslet. Although the main plot is regarded by many as being a little fanciful, the personal story of codebreakers who fall in love at Bletchley Park is none other than the story of Mavis and Keith, who discussed the film during its production with the director and stars and were guests of honour at the premiere.

Bletchley Park

Commander Denniston had been busy since the time of the Munich crisis in the early autumn of 1938. He had been building a list of 'available emergency staff', which consisted of professors and other academics at Cambridge and Oxford Universities, together with a group of 'old members', meaning codebreakers who had served with him in World War I. Denniston even had recourse to the newspapers, placing an advertisement for a professional mathematician. The notice was answered by Peter Twinn, a recently-graduated Oxford physicist, who was put straight onto the GC&CS payroll and joined Dilly Knox. The emergency staff were the reserve force to be called upon if a war were to begin – the assumption being that far more codebreaking would be needed than in times of peace.

Among the available emergency staff on Denniston's list was one A.M. Turing, from Cambridge, who was brought in, together with eight other academics, in early January 1939 to attend a course on codes and ciphers. The four-day 'short course' was taught by Denniston himself, together with Captain Tiltman and other senior GC&CS figures. The academic students learned about transposition ciphers, subtractor ciphers which disguised numerical codes, 'book-building' (meaning reconstructing a numerical code-book), and operational intelligence. There was no module devoted to cipher machines, but the practical work assigned to Turing was 'Enigma'.

Exactly what practical work that was remains unclear, but since Britain's knowledge of the German military version of Enigma was swathed in fog at the time one assumes it was a tutorial from Knox using the 'breaking machines, have you got a pencil' scheme. For the next six months, when Alan Turing was not doing his day-job of writing papers on mathematical logic, he was trying to fathom out the mysteries of the Enigma machine.

One day in late July or early August 1939, Alan Turing paid a visit to the home of Dilly Knox. The two men knew each other well, since they were both fellows of King's College, Cambridge, and after Turing's induction into the secrets of the GC&CS the relationship strengthened. Knox found Turing exasperating, because new ideas would fly off tangentially during their conversations – Knox blamed Turing for this, but it seems likely that the creativity, and disorder, was common to both of them. But in the summer of 1939 Knox had to make Turing sit and listen. For he had just returned from Poland, and had important information to give.

Dilly Knox described Marian Rejewski's theoretical attack on the Enigma wiring. Since that meeting in Warsaw, Knox had been sceptical about this, but Alan Turing was able to verify that Rejewski's mathematical approach was indeed a way to uncover the secret. No doubt there was some chagrin that the British had not discovered the

Alastair Denniston.

mathematical way for themselves, but now – and especially after the delivery of the precious Polish reconstruction of a German military Enigma machine, brought over from Paris by Bertrand – they were in a position to devote all their energy to the question of finding the daily settings used by the Germans to configure the machine: the choice and location of rotors, the plugboard connections, the ring-settings on the rotors, and the rotary orientation of each rotor. There was still a lot they couldn't know, and all of it changed every day, on every network.

Alan Turing – architect of the Bombe

The story of Alan Turing is now so well known it hardly needs to be re-told. Indeed, in the popular imagination, the story of Enigma is the story of Alan Turing; the story of Alan Turing is the story of Bletchley Park; all codebreaking is conflated into an Enigma-Bletchley-Turing triptych of almost religious symbolism. Perhaps a reappraisal is, after all, worthwhile.

Alan Turing was born in 1912 and studied mathematics at Cambridge University, where in 1935 he wrote a groundbreaking paper called *On Computable Numbers*, which laid the foundations for later computer development. On being called up for Alastair Denniston's reserve list, and attending a basic course for recruits 'of the professor type' in early 1939, he began working on the Enigma problem. But as a part-timer and without knowing the all-important wiring of the machine, he made no progress until after Knox and Denniston came back from Warsaw in July of that year. Now, armed with the results of the Polish codebreakers, he was able to put together his design for the British Bombe, which was mature enough to go to the engineers in the autumn.

All this means that Alan Turing's most important attack on Enigma was completed before Britain found itself in a fighting war, which began in earnest the following year. Certainly, that was not the end of his career as a codebreaker, but his other achievements and contributions seem small in comparison with the prolific output and significance of the Bombe. Those other contributions to pure cryptanalysis became fewer as time went on, and Turing became more of a consultant than a front-line codebreaker. By 1942 his original role was essentially over, so he was despatched first to the United States to liaise with the Americans on their efforts against Enigma, and, perhaps more significantly, to encrypt human speech. Speech encryption and cipher security were what occupied Alan Turing for the remainder of the war, so that he was not even resident at Bletchley Park after his return from the United States. Enigma was not his occupation any more.

After the war, Turing's career moved into computing machine development, strongly influenced by his experiences at Bletchley and beyond as to the capabilities of modern technology. Machine development and programming were intimately interwoven in those days. In the final years of his career he turned to the problems of shape and pattern development in living things, using the Manchester University computer to test out his theories.

All this, apart from the Bletchley episode, is overshadowed in the public mind by the tragedy of Alan Turing's final years. In 1952 he fell foul of the anti-homosexual purge instigated by the personalities then controlling the Home Office and the police, leading to a bizarre course of 'therapy' which required him to wear a synthetic oestrogen implant for a year. In 1954 he took his own life in circumstances which are still not fully understood. Unsurprisingly, the two incidents are linked in most people's minds, although no causal relationship can be proved. What is plain, though, on any reading, is that Alan Turing's tragic end coupled with the achievement at Bletchley made possible by the Bombe makes for a compelling story, and a great plot for a Hollywood epic.

The mansion house at Bletchley Park, the wartime home of the codebreakers.

All too soon the emergency which Denniston had prepared for became a reality. Prime Minister Chamberlain's declaration of war followed hard on the invasion of Poland by Germany. Instructions went out to the professors to gather at GC&CS's war site, to which the permanent staff had begun to migrate on 15 August 1939. The 'war site' was a 'mansion', a word which gives a wholly false impression of what was a modest manor house of the Victorian era. The mansion was a collage of incongruous architectural oddities, acquired by the Secret Intelligence Service (SIS) the year before as a suitable out-of-town location to which the Service, and its codebreaking subsidiary GC&CS, could be evacuated to escape the dangers of bombing while remaining in good communication with their political masters. It was called Bletchley Park, and it was wholly unsuited to house a high-tech and growing establishment.

The house at Bletchley Park was not large. The downstairs rooms, set aside for the codebreakers (apart from the areas needed for the caterers), consisted of a small office for Denniston and his personal assistant, the library, the billiard room, the ballroom and the morning room. The large dining room was also available, but people needed to eat somewhere. All this space, and more, was needed by the existing permanent staff, comprising well over a hundred people, who had moved up from London. Upstairs was occupied by both the SIS and a wireless intercept facility. Denniston's emergency, during what proved to be the 'phoney war' (unless you were unfortunate enough to be in Poland or at sea), was an emergency of accommodation.

Knox, Twinn, Turing and a handful of recruits hastily assembled to work on the Enigma problem could not fit into the space inside the mansion. For the time being, they were placed in the stable yard, where there were cottages which had once housed staff working for the gentry who owned the estate before the SIS. Since the site had been evacuated, apart from the caretaker and his family, the cottages were empty and could be used as codebreakers' working space. The cottages were cramped and noisy, and the sources of distraction were multiplied as carpenters and builders moved onto the site. Denniston's solution to the problem of space was to install wooden huts, of the pattern used for Scott's and Shackleton's explorations of Antarctica, in the gardens of the Park: over the coming months and years, more and more of the grounds were destined to be ripped up to make way for the huts, then brick-and-concrete blocks, a canteen, a teleprinter communications hub, a transportation hub, and more. That some of the original garden features such as the ornamental lake and the tennis-courts survived the devastation is remarkable.

Meanwhile, some of the professors were less fortunate still in their accommodation. Gordon Welchman, another mathematician from Cambridge, arrived to find himself 'banished' to the premises of the school whose premises abutted Bletchley Park. His assignment was to work on 'traffic analysis', or what these days would be described as the metadata surrounding messages. A lot of information could be gleaned from traffic analysis, since units tended to have identifying call-signs, which could be analysed to visualize enemy troop movements. Classifying Enigma traffic also simplified the attack on Enigma, since each network used its own 'key' or basic sheet of settings for the choice of rotors, ring-settings, and cross-pluggings; the metadata on messages such as the address code ensured that the intended recipients could pick out the signals which were intended to reach them and this information, conveniently, told the traffic analysers which network, which key, they were dealing with. All the messages sent in the same key would share basic Enigma set-up data.

Still, from Denniston's perspective, Enigma was going to be a huge challenge. It was a 'research' problem rather than an actual,

Alan Turing.

current source of intelligence. Indeed, almost twelve months into the war, Denniston was heard to say, 'You know, the Germans don't mean you to read their stuff, and I don't suppose you ever will.' Admittedly, that comment was made about German Naval Enigma, which was a more difficult problem than army and air force Enigma, but it indicates just how high the mountain was that needed to be climbed. It doesn't mean that Denniston was defeatist, just that he had to pursue the Enigma question as a sideline rather than the more fruitful sources of intelligence which were more immediately tractable.

It was clear to Denniston as much as to everyone else that the German military Enigma was going to need a mechanical solution, along Polish lines, and that the mathematicians recently hired by the GC&CS should lead the attack. To begin with, a suitable engineering firm was needed, since GC&CS had no manufacturing or workshop capability and no trained engineers. The search and implementation was delegated to the energetic and forceful Edward Travis, Denniston's deputy, whose skills were more aligned with management and getting things done than in the intellectual niceties of puzzle-solving. Travis connected with the BTM company in Letchworth, a firm which made punched-card computing machinery and had not only workshops but a track-record in inventive solutions to their customers' problems. Preserving secrecy, Travis used the White Hart Hotel in Buckingham as his notional address, to which BTM initially sent their letters. After various meetings, tentatively the GC&CS placed orders for machines; the mechanization of codebreaking had begun.

One option was to recreate the Polish method of searching for repeated letters in the indicator sequences of Enigma messages, using duplicates of their bomba device. But to encipher the indicator twice, as the Germans had been doing up till now, was an insecure practice; sooner or later, it was assumed, they would change their working methods, and the bomba would become obsolete overnight. What was needed was an attack on the Enigma set-up which did not depend on the indicator sequence.

Knox's training as a codebreaker, and his successes with the simpler Model K Enigma machine, pointed the way. The answer was to use the method of the 'probable word' or 'crib' to find a way in. While the Polish bomba searched for an Enigma rotor orientation which could consistently encipher 'females' – the repeats found in three messages' indicator sequences – an alternative method would be to check whether an Enigma rotor orientation could consistently encipher the letters of a probable word into an encrypted message intercepted over the wireless. Polish bombas searched exhaustively through all 17,576 rotor orientations, and stopped if there was one which could give the three observed repeats; a British version might be adapted to work with cribs, also searching exhaustively through all 17,576 rotor orientations, and stopping if there was one which could turn the crib consistently into the observed ciphertext.

This borrowing from the Poles was at the heart of the GC&CS's major technological experiment. Polish bombas used electro-mechanical wheels which imitated the rotor-banks of six Enigma machines. But the British machine was going to be much larger. Since the probable word might have many letters, the new machine would need to imitate the rotor-banks of far more Enigma machines. Together with BTM, the British were going to build a giant version of the bomba. They were going to build a Bombe.

By 1 November 1939, the Enigma team (Knox, Twinn, Welchman, Turing and John Jeffreys, another recruit who was to command the assault based on a set of Zygalski's punched cardboard sheets) reported on the Enigma position. First, the good news: 'we have enough Enigmas'. GC&CS had ordered and obtained replicas of Enigma machines, thanks to the gift of the reconstructed Enigma machine handed over by the Poles. There were also two cyclometers, the devices invented for spotting the 'characteristic' patterns of behaviour of particular rotor combinations; there were punches for making the holes in the cardboard sheets; and, most exciting of all, 'a large 30 enigma bomb machine, adapted to use for cribs, is on order and parts are being made at the British Tabulating Company.'

While the 30-Enigma giant Bombe might remove the dependency on the doubly-enciphered indicator, there was still a phenomenally difficult problem in adapting the Polish technology. This was the challenge of the plugboard incorporated into the German military version of Enigma. From 1 January 1939, the number of cables used to connect the terminals in the plugboard had been increased to ten: only six letters of the 26 in the alphabet would reach the Enigma rotors without having been changed by the plugboard. The implication was that a crib-based attack on the plugboard Enigma was bound to fail. For example, if the probable word is **BERIQT** (German telegraphese for '*Bericht*', meaning 'report'; sometimes **Q** was used in place of **CH**), and the daily key-sheet says that the plugboard cross-pluggings are **AV, BI, CJ, DP, EM, FK, GQ, HU, SZ** and **TY** (as in the key-sheet on page 25), the correct rotor orientation would generate IMRBGY, which is nothing like BERIQT. Somehow, the British Bombe needed to search for plugboard cabling as well as rotor orientation.

Alan Turing's imagination and inventiveness came to bear on the problem at this point. He recognized that testing for the rotor orientation could be done without knowing the plugboard connections. By connecting combinations of letters derived from the crib and ciphertext into loops, electrical circuit diagrams called 'menus' could be constructed which would enable such a test to take place. To enable the test to run, a guess would need to be made as to how one letter featured in the menu might have been connected

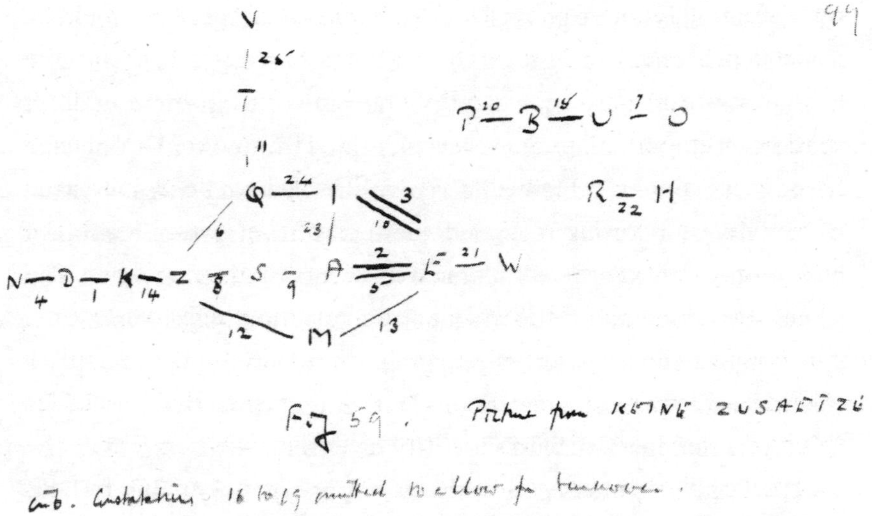

99

V
| 26
T
| 11
Q $\frac{22}{23}$ | | $\frac{3}{10}$ R $\frac{}{72}$ H

P $\frac{20}{}$ B $\frac{18}{}$ U $\frac{2}{}$ O

/ 6

N $\frac{}{4}$ D $\frac{}{1}$ K $\frac{}{14}$ Z $\frac{}{8}$ S $\frac{}{9}$ A $\frac{2}{5}$ E $\frac{21}{}$ W

/ 12   M / 13

Fig 59 .   Picture from KEINE ZUSAETZE

arb. Constatation 16 to 19 omitted to allow for turnover.

A menu designed by Alan Turing.

up on the plugboard. If that guess was right, then a British Bombe machine could test for the rotor positions.

Of course, one guess out of 26 for that vital plugboard connection was a long shot. What was really needed was a Bombe machine which could test all 26 possible plugboard connections at the same time – a machine which, in the Bombe design team's jargon, could do 'simultaneous scanning'. Once again, Turing's imagination came to the rescue. The simple guess for one plugboard connection would be translated, in engineering terms, into a voltage applied to a single wire in a 26-wire cable: the equivalent of choosing one letter out of 26. If the correct rotor configuration was identified by the Bombe, only one wire in the 26-wire cable would remain live, with 25 wires showing no activity. But Turing reckoned there was an inverse situation: if all but one wire went live, the inactive twenty-sixth wire would also signal something about the plugboard connection guess – in fact, it could signal the actual cross-plugging, even if the operator's guess was wrong. It was just a matter of identifying the inactive wire in the cable, and that inactive wire's identifying letter.

The Bombe as envisaged in this way was not only going to have more sophisticated logic than its Polish progenitor, but much more challenging engineering. Turing's 'hot wire' and 'cold wire' solution required a novel system of relays which could stop the machine in either of these situations, but allow it to continue running if all wires ran hot. Fortunately, Turing's imagination as to the theory was matched by the imagination of BTM's chief engineer, Harold 'Doc' Keen, who was able to devise real circuitry which implemented the idea. And all this was done by 1 November 1939, when Knox and the others in his Bombe team provided their progress report to the GC&CS hierarchy.

The Bombe – how it works

The purpose of the Bombe was to find some (not all) of the settings used to encipher a particular Enigma message: the orientation of the rotors when the first letter of the message was enciphered, and one of the plugboard cross-wirings. The rest would have to be found by guesswork (which three rotors to test, and in which order they were, for example) or analysis after the Bombe completed its run (the rest of the plugboard wirings, and the ring settings). There was no guarantee that the Bombe would have found the correct solution: it was merely offering a plausible possibility for further testing. But the further analysis was manageable in a short enough period for the Bombe operators to divine the actual Enigma settings in a very short while, short enough for the production of intelligence which was up-to-date and useful.

The front of the Bombe is where rotor-like 'drums', emulating the behaviour of the different Enigma rotors, were installed in banks of three just as in an Enigma machine. These were connected up to each other, using 26-wire cables. Each set of three pseudo-Enigmas would test the encryption of a selected letter of the message. The cabling connecting the pseudo-Enigmas together was configured according to a diagram called a 'menu', constructed from letter-pairs in a comparison of the 'crib' (probably plain-text content of the message) and the intercepted ciphertext.

To take an actual example used by Alan Turing to explain the method, imagine that the plain text is believed to contain the words **KEINE ZUSAETZE ZUM VORBERIQT** ('nothing to add to preliminary report'), and the intercepted text was **DAEDAQOZSIQMMKEILGMPWHAIV**. By lining up the crib and intercept texts we can find pairs of letters which chain together:

K	E	I	N	E	Z	U	S	A	E	T	Z	E	Z	U	M	V	O	R	B	E
D	A	E	D	A	Q	O	Z	S	I	Q	M	M	K	E	I	L	G	M	P	W
				5			8	9			12	13								

The pairs were called 'constatations'. The constatation at position 5 implies that **E** became enciphered as **A**. Then, at position 9, **A** became enciphered as **S**, and at position 8, **S** was enciphered as **Z**. Putting all the shaded constatations together we can build a chain **E→A→S→Z→M→E**. Other chains using other constatations can also be built; what was particularly useful here is that the chain loops back on itself, finishing with **E**, where it started. Each arrow in the chain represents the transformation carried out by the rotors of the Enigma machine, or (the same thing) a bank of three drums on the Bombe. Here, five banks of drums offset to correspond to five, eight, nine, twelve and thirteen positions from the message's start position can be connected up into a loop, to form an electrical circuit. Loops like this were built up to create a 'menu' for connecting up the cabling on the Bombe, with each connection-point representing a letter in the menu.

Electricity is introduced into one wire of the 26-wire cables linking the pseudo-Enigmas. The chosen wire represents the codebreaker's guess as to how the plugboard is connected for that letter: so, if the guess is that **E** is plugged to **X**, a switch on the end of the Bombe will be thrown to apply a voltage to the **X** wire at position **E** on the menu, which is one of the connection points where the pseudo-Enigmas are joined together by cabling.

Now the Bombe can be switched on to run. Working through all 17,576 combinations of rotor orientation, the machine will stop when a rotor configuration leaves only one wire in the 26-wire cable live, and electricity fails to reach the other wires. The purity of the single electrical circuit through all the cabling and rotors implies that a correct rotor orientation has been found, which could consistently encipher all chosen letters from the message in the observed way. It also implies that the guess about the cross-plugging was also correct. If electricity reaches other wires, the path taken was not the one envisaged by the menu, where electricity should travel in a pure circuit around the loop and not reach other letters or wires. Multiple live wires implied a bad rotor orientation, so the Bombe would move the rotors on swiftly to test another configuration.

But the machine can also stop if electricity *fails* to reach a single wire. That is also an example of electrical circuit purity, which also indicates a correct rotor orientation; but because the voltage was not applied to that pure circuit, the cross-plugging must have been wrongly guessed. In this case, the Bombe substitutes its own story: the inactive wire at the menu position will be signalled to the operator in the small indicator panel next to the switch-bank on the end of the Bombe.

Thus, if the Bombe stops, it tells the operator – via the bronze-coloured indicator drums at the right-hand end of the middle row of drum-banks – what rotor configuration might have been used at the beginning of encryption, and what cross-plugging might have been used at the beginning of encryption, and what cross-plugging might have been used for one letter in the menu.

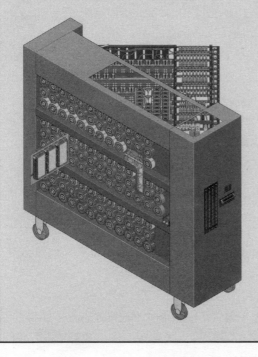

*A schematic drawing
of the Bombe.*

The winter of 1939-40 was icy cold. The ornamental lake at Bletchley froze over, and intrepid codebreakers teetered gingerly over the ice on skates. In the world of Enigma, by contrast, things were warming up. The Polish codebreakers had, almost miraculously, turned up in France, where Gustave Bertrand had installed them as part – in fact, the majority – of his team. This was a cue for a new row starring Dilly Knox, who was now firmly in favour of the Polish effort against Enigma and complained loudly that the British were not assisting them. The principal bone of contention was the supply of punched cardboard sheets on the Zygalski model. Now that the sheets were available in Britain, it was a matter of duty and honour to supply a set to the Poles in Paris, and Knox volunteered to take them over himself if this was the way to break the deadlock. Denniston prudently decided that Knox's talents were better deployed at Bletchley, and sent Alan Turing instead.

Turing's visit to Paris – the only recorded instance of a meeting between Turing and the Poles – took place on 17 January 1940. His role was not only that of courier, but to receive a tutorial on the use of the sheets – not a trivial matter – and to clear up a query relating to the two new rotors which the Germans had introduced twelve months before. For some reason the British were in a muddle about the location of the turnover notch on these new rotors, a minor confusion which was quickly cleared up.

Armed with a set of sheets the Poles could now turn again to the decryption of Enigma messages. Within 24 hours of the arrival of the Zygalski sheets the first break was made: it was of an old intercept, dating from 28 October 1939, and of no imaginable use – but that wasn't the point. The Poles could break Enigma, and using the same technique, so could the British. The first British break was achieved on 20 January, as soon as Bletchley Park learned what Turing had been told. Again, the message broken was out of date (25 October

1939) and, from an intelligence perspective, quite useless. But at least the teams on both sides of the Channel were now working, effectively, and able to see what the Germans were saying.

Bertrand moved his team out of central Paris to occupy a somewhat exotic château in the village of Gretz-Armainvilliers, close enough to Paris for good communications but, with luck, away from danger. Liaison with Bletchley was established through a teleprinter line. As soon as keys (Enigma setting information) were identified, they were transmitted across. Success bred success: new insights into the way German operators would cut corners sped up the way that keys could be found.

- 'Cillies' were giveaways. Although operators were supposed to pick letters at random for the 'ground-setting', the part of the message 'indicator' which told the receiver how to set the rotors for the deciphering of the 'message setting', they didn't. Often, they would choose real words which gave away the secret message setting without needing to know anything other than how to complete a six-letter word. So a ground-setting **HIT** followed by three enciphered letters **JPY** might well imply the complete indicator **HIT-LER**, telling Bletchley Park that with the rotors in initial position **HIT** the letters **LER** are enciphered as **JPY**: a crib, and one which might happily enable the rest of the key to come out. Other common 'cillies' were sequences found on the Enigma keyboard (**ASD-FGH**) or frequently used military abbreviations.
- The 'Herivel tip' was the fruit of a Bletchley Park codebreaker's insight into other ways operators might cut corners. Although rotor choices and ring-settings would be changed every day, an operator putting in the rotors for

the first time would set the clip on the ring, and like as not the rotor's orientation in the machine would have the ring-clip uppermost or only one or two places away. Then the operator, lost for a choice of a random three-letter sequence for the day's first ground-setting, would look through the viewing windows and use the visible letters. The first three letters of any day's first message thus told Bletchley Park (and the team at Gretz-Armainvilliers) the likely rotor choice and order and the ring settings – a massive saving on testing of different permutations.

- The 'Method Knox' was so named by the Franco-Polish team in honour of Dilly, who presumably discovered it; it exploited German laziness in another form. It was especially useful for multi-part messages where the second and subsequent parts should have been enciphered at freshly chosen settings. But lazy operators would save time by using the rotor letters visible in their Enigma machine's viewing windows at the end of the previous message-part – as the ground-setting for the next part. Worse, the operators re-used the original message setting for all parts of the message, which could be revealed simply by turning the rotors backwards from the lazily-chosen ground-setting for part 2 by the number of letters in part 1. The Poles noted that the Method Knox was particularly valuable when the war began in earnest in Western Europe during the Norway campaign, which erupted in the spring of 1940.

By the time of the outbreak of hostilities in the West, an organizational plan for breaking and exploiting Enigma had been devised by Gordon Welchman. First, he proposed colour-coding the different networks being used for Enigma signals. Then, there should be a distinction between the cryptanalytic effort – finding cribs and keys – and the translation, processing and exploitation of the contents of broken messages. The structure Welchman envisioned led to the creation of Bletchley Park's famous Hut system: Huts 3 and 6, for German Army and air force Enigma (where Hut 3 did the interpretive work, and Hut 6 the cryptanalysis), and Huts 4 and 8, for German Naval Enigma (again, interpretation and cryptanalysis respectively). Naval Enigma was a species apart from Army and Air Force Enigma, with more complex key arrangements, and is discussed in the next chapter.

Welchman also had a key role in the development of Alan Turing's supercharged Bombe machine. The much-awaited prototype was delivered to Bletchley on 18 March 1940, and installed in Hut 1, just across the tennis courts outside the Mansion building. It worked just fine. Or rather, it worked a bit too well: the Bombe stopped many times during a run, each stop indicating that it had found a possible rotor start-position consistent with the 'menu' or testing-programme which it had been set. The problem was that a minimum of three closed loops were needed to make a good menu and minimize the number of 'stops', and these were very hard to come by even with convincing cribs.

While the Bombe team were wringing their hands over this, the temperature of the war was coming towards boiling. In April, Germany invaded Denmark and Norway. A botched campaign to eject the Germans from Norway ended with the fall of the British Government led by Neville Chamberlain and the installation of Winston Churchill as prime minister. The Germans invaded the Netherlands, Belgium and France. The French Army was unable to repeat its stolid resistance of the previous war, and things looked very bleak for Britain. Subsequent analysis would show that the fiasco of Norway was in part attributable to the immaturity of intelligence and counter-intelligence structures: while the Germans had good insight into British intentions, the information gleaned by the British and French was either poorly interpreted or ignored by the military commanders. Against this backdrop, whatever the Enigma codebreakers could do with the limited tools they had – cillies, Method Knox, Herivel's tip, and occasional Bombe results – made little impact. Then, on 1 May 1940, the expected change of German Enigma operating procedure came into effect: no longer would they encipher the three-letter 'message setting' twice over. From then on it would be enciphered once only, ruining the techniques invented by the Poles, such as cyclometers and Zygalski sheets.

But what the war was showing was that Welchman was right on the organizational side of things. Received wisdom, which is to say the emanations of wiser, greyer heads of the previous conflict, held that when the fighting began the use of radio would stop, owing to its insecurity. Not so: the increase in Enigma traffic spinning through the airwaves was astronomic. What the Allies needed was an industrial-scale solution, to capture the signals, decrypt them, and turn them into much-needed intelligence. The solution would have to be the Bombe, and it needed an upgrade.

Gordon Welchman's inventiveness came to the fore once again, this time in the field of machine logic. He suggested adding a simple supplementary cross-wiring device to the machine, which would artificially create a vast number of additional loops for even simple menus. He figured that the plugboard on Enigma machines was reciprocal: if **A** was plugged to **W** then **W** was plugged to **A**. Translating this into electrical circuitry, this meant that if the **A** wire was live at point **W** in a menu, the **W** wire should be live at point **A** in the same menu. A simple 'diagonal board' could connect the reciprocal wires, and would be easy to insert into the machine. At first, Alan Turing was incredulous; but he saw the brilliance of Welchman's suggestion, and the engineers were set to work to upgrade the electro-mechanical device which was, ultimately, to prove fatal to the security of German Enigma.

During the summer of 1940, the Germans turned their attention from France to the elimination of Britain, their sole undefeated adversary. Enigma decrypts confirmed their plan to eradicate the Royal Air Force before mounting an amphibious assault across the Channel. Fortunately, cillies were still producing a small but useful trickle of messages from the Luftwaffe's key named 'Red' by the traffic analysts. Together with metadata analysis the intelligence officers could infer a pattern of German intentions, enough to help stave off the threat day by day.

Eventually, on 8 August 1940, a modified Turing-Welchman Bombe arrived at Bletchley. Straightaway it was put to work on the 'Red' key; straightaway the machine, named 'Agnes' or 'Agnus Dei', proved her worth. The number of stops was manageable, and the previous successes with 'Red' gave a collection of likely cribs to enable menus to be set up. It was just in time. The Blitz – Germany's strategic bombing campaign against British targets – began in earnest in September 1940, and the aerial war over Britain came to a peak that month. Meanwhile, the old prototype Bombe was refitted with a diagonal board, and came into service in September. This one was called 'Victory', since Enigma intelligence was turning, if not into a flood just yet, at least a fast-flowing stream.

Gordon Welchman: the real Enigma codebreaker

The breaking of Enigma at Bletchley Park is imagined to be the work mainly of one man, Alan Turing. Yet Alan Turing's input to the design of the Bombe machine, while original and brilliant, was not enough to create the astonishing success that Bletchley Park made of the voluminous Enigma material.

In the first place, Alan Turing's Bombe was too weak to reduce the number of possible permutations to a manageable number. It took Gordon Welchman's diagonal board to achieve that – which is why the rebuilt Bombe at The National Museum of Computing celebrates both these inventors equally.

But Gordon Welchman's talents went far beyond the computing logic involved in his enhancement to the Bombe. It was his organizational approach which set up the 'Hut System', ordering the somewhat chaotic approach of the pre-war codebreakers who liked to do every step of a codebreaking process themselves, following an intercept all the way through to translation and interpretation. That this was inefficient and duplicative, and a waste of talent, was evident to Welchman from a very early stage, so he presented his organizational plan to Commander Travis at Bletchley at around the time the Bombe machine was being developed – even then, Welchman had the vision that Enigma volumes were going to skyrocket and a specific Enigma sub-organization at Bletchley would be essential.

The Hut System devised by Welchman survived until the end of the war, beyond the point at which Welchman himself had been promoted to Assistant Director (Mechanisation), which took him away from Hut 6 and put him in charge of all things to do with machinery at Bletchley Park. This made him the chief resolver of periodic priority crises whenever there was not enough equipment to go around – not enough Bombes, not enough Typex machines, not enough Hollerith punched-card equipment – and development of new machines stretched the human and material resources even further. Towards the end of the war Welchman, like Turing, was awarded the OBE.

The story of Gordon Welchman has an unhappy twist at the end. In 1982, towards the end of his life, he wrote up his own account of the Bletchley years, *The Hut Six Story*, which contained an explanation of the basic ideas of Enigma codebreaking. Although much in the book had already been revealed, and nobody could imagine that an enemy could benefit in the 1980s from technical information about an encryption machine which was ancient history, Welchman was stripped of his security clearance and ostracized from the intelligence community. Welchman's crime was that he had been at Bletchley Park and bound by the code of silence which was supposed to endure forever.

'We do not expect outsiders to show any great sense of responsibility in what they publish, but you can perhaps understand that it is a bitter blow to us, as well as a disastrous example to others, when valued ex-colleagues decide to let us down.' This schoolmasterish reprimand, from the pen of Sir Peter Marychurch, head of GCHQ (Government Communications Headquarters, home of modern British intelligence-gathering), might be thought too ridiculous to take seriously. But for Welchman it was much more significant. He had been trying to do the right thing by the Byzantine and anachronistic official rules of secrecy relating to the wartime activities of Bletchley Park; after all, he was not the only one writing memoirs or the first to expose what had happened there. He had been through the 'proper channels', or so he thought, and yet his own security clearance had been revoked on the basis that he was a security risk – just like Alan Turing.

The fighters' success in the Battle of Britain did not mean the end of Germany's bombing campaign, even if the planned invasion was postponed. German technology had created a special targeting system, using crossing radio beams to home the bombers on to their targets. A different Enigma key, christened 'Brown' at Bletchley Park, gave the instructions for the beam system. 'Brown' was attacked with the two cryptanalytic Bombes, enabling the beams to be jammed and disrupting the bombs of the explosive type. It wasn't always fool-proof, and despite the efforts of Bletchley's codebreakers the city of Coventry was all but wiped out in a night of destruction on 14 November (see box opposite).

Coventry proved little other than that codebreaking is not fool-proof: all the circumstances, and a great deal of additional knowledge, might be needed to build a complete intelligence picture. The picture would, however, be a great deal more complete if the volume of material were increased, and every detail logged and cross-referenced. So began a tedious process of capturing every atom of data gleaned from broken Enigma messages – useless bits of information which had no value for current operations, but which might help with pattern identification, in the business of creating useable cribs, and eventually clues to impossible problems like the codenames given by the Germans to towns like Coventry.

Gustave Bertrand's operation at Gretz-Armainvilliers had been forced to close when the German invasion of France got too close. He bundled up his team of Polish codebreakers and evacuated them to French North Africa, before re-inserting them into France clandestinely to continue the struggle in the unoccupied part of the country after the Franco-German armistice. In 1943 some of them would fetch up in Britain, followed in 1944 by Bertrand himself, but following the French defeat the centre of gravity on Enigma codebreaking shifted irreversibly to Bletchley. Within a year or so of the fall of France, Bletchley had succeeded in Gordon Welchman's mission of industrializing the attack on Enigma.

But what these statistics do not reveal is the snail-like progress in the attack on Naval Enigma. Naval messages are not included in these numbers, because Naval Enigma was a much greater challenge than that posed by the German Army and air force. The problem could not be ignored, because by the end of 1940 the Battle of the Atlantic had begun in earnest, and the survival of Britain, once threatened from the air, was now in peril on the sea.

The myth of Coventry

The tragedy of Coventry's bombing in November 1940 has become perverted into an unattractive myth, that Winston Churchill allowed the city to be destroyed in order to protect the secret that Enigma was being broken.

The myth seems to have begun when, in 1974, the achievements at Bletchley Park were first revealed to the public in a bestselling book called *The Ultra Secret*, by F.W. Winterbotham, a senior air intelligence officer who had a good deal of personal knowledge about Bletchley and its product, but no access to official sources. Winterbotham says, quite rightly, that the German signals identifying targets were being read, and that the actual targets were specified using codenames rather than being spelt out. However, he says that

The city centre of Coventry after the bombing. Despite popular belief, the UK government didn't allow Coventry to be attacked to preserve the codebreaking secret – they were simply unaware that Coventry was the target described in the message.

in the case of Coventry no codename was used, that the identity of the target was given to Churchill's staff, and that a decision was taken not to evacuate the city but only to warn the emergency services. His account concludes by saying 'Official history maintains that the Air Ministry had two days' notice of this raid.' It appears to be an indictment.

Curiously, the Official History was actually written after Winterbotham's book, with the relevant volume being published only in 1979. The attack on Coventry is covered in three pages of the main text and a 20-page appendix setting out the state of knowledge and the decisions in painful detail. In summary, an Enigma decrypt indeed disclosed on 11 November, two days before the raid, that the German radio beams were to be directed on a target code-named 'Korn'. It was obvious from the intelligence context that the operation was going to be massive, deploying every available long-range bomber, but what was the meaning of 'Korn'? Air intelligence identified some likely target areas, one of which was 'the industrial district of England', based on a prisoner-of-war interrogation which mentioned Birmingham and Coventry as possible targets. But there was no Enigma message containing the word Coventry and nobody guessed what Korn might actually mean. Churchill did not abandon Coventry and its inhabitants to their fate, because he did not know they were in Germany's sights, still less to protect the secret of Enigma codebreaking.

Between X and Y

The party from London who visited Warsaw in July 1939 comprised not only Alastair Denniston and Dilly Knox but a mysterious third man. The Polish hosts and the French guests understood this gentleman, who was sufficiently important to have travelled by air while the others had taken the slow route by train, to be 'Professor Sandwich'. The cover name was so obviously fake that speculation began at once. The smart money was on the 'professor' being Colonel Stewart Menzies, who at that time was the senior MI6 officer in charge of the GC&CS, and destined, within a few months, to become 'C', the head of the whole MI6 organization.

As with so many conspiracy theories the solution was more prosaic. The distinguished third man was not Menzies but Commander

Humphrey Sandwith. Sandwith was not a professor but a naval officer, whose specialism was radio interception. From the initial meeting in January, when the three countries' Enigma teams had conferred for the first time, it was obvious that little of cryptanalytical value was likely to emerge from the new conference; but one of the real benefits of the January meeting had been the gathering and sharing of intercepted German radio traffic. Sandwith was in Warsaw to consolidate and expand cooperation in the field of interception and distribution of undeciphered Morse code.

Collecting the raw ingredients without which the cookery of Bletchley Park would result in an empty plate was complex as well as vital. Late 1930s radio transmission was as much art as science. Transmitters wobbled in the volume of their output and did not keep to a steady frequency. Atmospheric conditions and sunspots made certain times of year and certain geographies useless for interception. Some places were mysterious blackout zones where no signal could be found. As the war began, and German forces spread themselves over vast areas of earth and sea, transmitting Enigma messages from wherever they were, more wireless interception masts were needed, and in as many places as possible. So the 'Y' service, a contraction of 'WI' or wireless interception service, came into being.

To begin with, there was Station X. At Bletchley Park itself, there was a water tower above the older part of the mansion building, reached by narrow stairs, with a small room beneath. The room was rigged as a radio receiving station, and a long aerial was strung from the tower to a tall cedar tree in the lawn to the front of the house. Another wire led to another tree by the lake, continuing via trees near the tennis courts and back to the tower to create a loop. But there was a problem: if Bletchley was to be a highly secret codebreaking site, masquerading for the benefit of inquisitive locals as something to do with the air defence of London, this rather obvious feature might be something of a giveaway, and might even constitute a target. The aerial was dismantled and the wireless operators moved up the road to Whaddon Hall. A more organized network of Y stations was needed.

Bletchley Park and the GC&CS might have been exemplary for inter-service coordination and sharing of facilities and expertise, but the cooperation did not extend beyond cryptanalysis. Collection of the all-important signals was considered by each of the services to be a proprietary consideration, a chaotic arrangement which caused headaches for the codebreakers throughout the war. The Royal Navy, the Royal Air Force, the Army and the Diplomatic Service each wanted to control the gathering of material which their specific interests demanded. The General Post Office, which had regulatory oversight and control of telecommunications, had their own operation. So did the Metropolitan Police. And then there was the Radio Security Service, set up specifically to track down illicit wireless transmissions from within the United Kingdom (and which, later in the war, would go on to eavesdrop on signals emanating overseas from undercover agents, as well as provide a range of fascinating and clandestine support services in various fields after the manner of 'Q Division' in the James Bond stories). Coordination was one thing, however, that was absent among all this activity.

All this left the codebreakers at Bletchley Park, who considered that they were the consumers of the intercepted signals, feeling ignored and something of a nuisance. Getting the Enigma traffic – getting the Y services to focus on Enigma traffic, which was the source relied on to provide cryptanalytic intelligence – was absurdly hard. The historian of codebreaking Ralph Erskine learned that 'when Josh Cooper, the head of [Bletchley Park's] Air Section, suggested that an RAF station should take Enigma, the head of the RAF Y service told him "My Y Service exists to produce intelligence, not to provide stuff for people at Bletchley to fool about with."'

There was a reason why the RAF thought that 'intelligence' came direct from the Y service rather than Bletchley, and it was not just that by denying Bletchley access to intercepts they were depriving themselves of the fruits of Enigma decryption. Much useful information came from direction-finding and 'traffic analysis', in other words the study of call signs (specific to particular units) and other metadata, whereas the ability to derive useful intelligence from the actual encrypted content of the signals no doubt seemed fanciful – especially to those who were not allowed to know that Bletchley Park was succeeding in its esoteric arts.

By 1941 the RAF had grasped the importance of the link to Bletchley, but the collection of intercepts was still at an early stage of development. Group Captain John Shephard was put in charge of the intercept station at Chicksands Priory in Bedfordshire. He was recovering from sickness and was led to believe the role would be something of a sinecure. Alas, he had not been told that

an embryo operation there already had to be expanded something like ten times by the day before yesterday. In ten months we built a camp for airmen – and airwomen – and a technical site to replace the spooky old Priory, and we trained a thousand or so wireless operators to provide Bletchley with some of the enormous mass of German Air Force high grade ciphers.

The intercept station at Chicksands saw its first complete day of monitoring Enigma messages slightly earlier, on 4 July 1940, when 262 messages were intercepted and sent to Bletchley. In January 1941, the interception team from Chatham was moved to Chicksands. From here on the focus was interception of Enigma messages. To begin with, Chicksands served all three of the armed forces, but by

Beaumanor Hall, the home of War Office Y Group.

the autumn interservice friction led to a split: Chicksands would be principally an air force site, with backup for the other two services, and the main Army Enigma interception operation was renamed the War Office Y Group (WOYG) and relocated to Beaumanor Hall in Leicestershire. (Beaumanor is an attractive large country house which now operates as a venue for weddings and conferences, but also offers tours showcasing its history as a World War II listening station.)

Teething problems for the listening service were manifold. Chicksands complained about a shortage of teleprinter lines and obtaining priority on their use over other service demands, the shortage of accommodation for staff, aerials which were installed without regard to the direction from which signals were coming, a shortage of spare parts and amplifiers, that German signals were being jammed by British radio signals and, above all, a shortage of staff. It wasn't only equipment and logistical problems that beset the Y service, either. The insatiable need for more staff led to the recruitment of young women who had joined the Auxiliary Territorial Service, or ATS. Commander Travis of Bletchley Park, looking back without nostalgia at the earlier days of radio interception, noted that:

> When the ATS first arrived at Beaumanor they were almost useless. The GAF [German Air Force] frequencies covered by Beaumanor were of 1st rate importance for the campaign in Egypt and could not be entrusted to them. The Army Groups were mostly too difficult.

Rapid expansion and cluelessness about what the job entailed impeded the selection and training of staff. After its troubled start, Beaumanor seems to have done better than Chicksands: 'Chicksands has been slow to learn how to handle women operators'; 'two essential

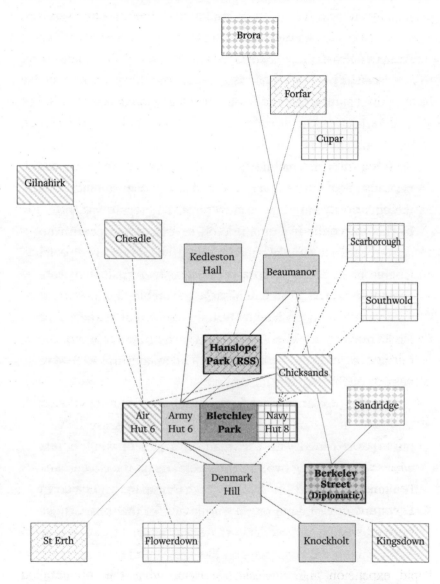

Major listening stations.

qualities of a ... Y station are flexibility and unorthodoxy; Chicksands seems to do well with the former, but are in my view run too much on "Service" lines to achieve the latter'.

Barbara Bairnsfather joined up in 1941. Having adjusted, or tried to, to a regimen of uncomfortable uniforms, worse-than-uncomfortable barracks and square-bashing, it was time for training:

One problem was that since the project was so secret the Y Signals authorities had not given the selection officers at the basic training camps a very clear idea of what qualifications the embryo operators needed to have. The result was that ... by the end of the five months' course, out of 24 women who started out in my intake only three of us went on to be Special Operators .... In May those of us who had graduated were posted to WOYG Beaumanor. HQ at Bletchley Park, (known as Station X) had established Beaumanor in 1941 as the HQ of No.6 Intelligence School, with an attached intercept station, manned by civilians from the Post Office, and the ATS were being brought in to replace them....

My first experience of operational duty was somewhat traumatic. It was on the evening shift, which was usually very busy. I was paired with a civilian on a pair of wireless sets which were covering two German operators on the Greenshank [Enigma] network (German Army High Command).... I sat down very nervously, and put on the earphones for the other set. He finished writing and suddenly there was a blur of morse code in my ears. It didn't sound a bit like the careful clear morse of the instructors at Trowbridge. My partner looked at me saying: 'Did you get that receipt?' Covered with shame I had to say: 'No'. He rolled his eyes to heaven in complete disgust and called the supervisor over and I was removed in disgrace and put on a 'Gannet' network from Norway which sent weather reports every four hours, which even an idiot couldn't screw up.

Major General Davidson, the Director of Military Intelligence no less, visited Beaumanor in August 1942 to consider the problems of staffing. At the time the 'wastage' of ATS servicewomen was over 50 per cent. A breakdown of the numbers told the following story:

675 ATS arrived for training
175 were wasted
    of the remainder
267 arrived WOYG
54 were wasted
70 were operational
143 still training at WOYG

What was needed was a shakeup, and a training programme which was focused on the needs of the service. The staff crisis was partly a legacy of a clash between the head of MI8 ('a new colonel who knows nothing about "E" traffic', according to Gordon Welchman – by 'E', Welchman meant 'Enigma') and Commander Ellingworth, who had established a good relationship with Welchman and turned the programme round. The colonel disappeared from the scene and Ellingworth's methods improved the quality of the service, as well as encouraging the ATS recruits.

Targeting traffic specifically encrypted with Enigma, rather than other types of cipher, was not straightforward, even when the organizational problems had been tackled. In January 1943 General Davidson advised, 'Naturally the various Services should be responsible for providing and maintaining these intercept stations but I feel it should be recognized that it is the responsibility of GC&CS

acting under the instructions of the Y Board ... to control the whole of their work.' Putting GC&CS in control was easier said than done, however. In March, Welchman was complaining that the Y service was still ignoring Bletchley Park's needs:

> The whole object of training operators in 'E' interception is to produce intelligence by breaking 'E' traffic. This is a highly technical matter about which GC&CS alone can speak with authority. The decision to transfer 38 of the best ATS operators from Beaumanor (to stations overseas) was taken without consultation with GC&CS, and a request for information was not even answered.

In order to be of use to the codebreakers at Bletchley, accuracy was of prime importance, so taking away the most experienced and precise operators threatened the effectiveness of Bletchley's own service. 'We had to get the preamble and the first three blocks absolutely accurate,' recorded Joan Nicholls, an ATS wireless operator, 'because that was the key to decoding the message. If we missed a letter we had to know exactly what position it was in and if the signal faded and we lost information, we had to know how many blocks we missed.' Operators listening in on Enigma traffic could not be treated as replaceable and interchangeable, and Bletchley – unlike the unsympathetic War Office – understood the problem. 'German Army traffic is more difficult to intercept than G.A.F. [German Air Force] traffic,' reported Gordon Welchman; moreover 'Army traffic is also more difficult to break; much more important therefore is it that the operators who are covering it shall be fully up to their job.'

The Y listeners faced numerous difficulties in carrying out their task. The wavelength on which the German transmitter sent the message could drift about, obliging the receiving unit – and anyone eavesdropping – to retune constantly, one hand on the tuning dial and one scribbling down the morse code letters on to a specially-designed pad. The weather and general atmospheric conditions could make the signal strength fall or crackle with interference. There were other stations broadcasting on nearby wavelengths – Barbara Bairnsfather recalled having to pick out a morse signal behind an operatic diva singing loudly in German. To make things worse, the Germans had ploys to catch out the eavesdroppers. Frequencies and call signs were changed daily at midnight on most networks, and the risk was that valuable sources might be lost. So interceptors had to keep tabs on the senders, listening to their chat as well as the encrypted signals. Chat and message preambles contained useful hints about what was happening, but perhaps the most useful thing was the 'fist', or characteristic style of an experienced morse code telegraphist.

The cartoonist's daughter

During World War I the talented draughtsman Bruce Bairnsfather was serving as a junior officer in Northern France, sharing the mud, cigarettes and continuous bombardment with the men under his command. The result was a series of published *Fragments from France* illustrating, with surprising good humour, the life of the Tommy in the trenches. The most famous cartoon was of two soldiers cowering in a shell-hole. One of the characters became known as 'Old Bill'; after the war, Old Bill became a subject for the theatre, taking the Tommy experience to towns all across Britain and even overseas.

In World War II, Bairnsfather served again, but this time his daughter was also in uniform. She joined the ATS in 1941, training as a radio interceptor. Her surname was instantly recognizable from her father's cartoons, which continued to appear. Whether this was a handicap Barbara Bairnsfather does not say; she was energetic, sporty and bright, and perfectly able to make her own way in the world. By 1943 she had been selected as an officer candidate, and part of her training involved a course at Bletchley, sleeping in a hut and eating in the officers' mess in the mansion. She became one of the first four ATS operational officers, posted to Harrogate to oversee junior ATS interceptors in the still-unfinished intercept station in the isolated and ominously named Blubberhouses Moor.

After the war, Barbara Bairnsfather emigrated to the United States, married and became a United States citizen in 1955. Like her father, Barbara was an accomplished artist and a canny observer, leaving not only an interesting and amusing memoir of her ATS experiences but some cartoons of her own.

"Well, if you knows of a better 'ole, go to it"

BY CAPT. BRUCE BAIRNSFATHER

A World War I cartoon by Bruce Bairnsfather.

As most people know, the alphabet is encoded in morse as a series of dots and dashes. To send a message using either a wired telegraph or wireless radio, the signaller created the dots and dashes by pressing on a sprung knob to close an electrical circuit, generating a pulse, or noise, or buzz, for as long as the circuit was closed. A dot meant releasing the knob as soon as possible, whereas a dash required the knob to be pressed down for longer. Spaces between letters needed to be longer than the spaces between individual dots and dashes making up a single letter. Each signaller would have his own particular idiosyncrasies in the length of dashes, or of the gaps, in the same way that speech patterns are characteristic of the speaker. Radio listeners could recognize the sender through the characteristic way in which the signaller 'spoke' when sending morse – this was known as the 'fist' of the sender. When a signalling unit switched to another frequency, a new call sign or even another location or a new transmitter, the fist of the signaller could give away the change and enable continuity of supply of the precious traffic from the unit in question.

An undulator tape record of morse code.

The skill of experienced interceptors in spotting the fist of the sender was inevitably vulnerable to the staff changes such as those which were upsetting Bletchley Park in 1943. One possible answer to this was to automate the process. A device called TINA (the explanations for the codename vary) allowed morse transmissions to be captured by an 'undulator' which recorded on paper tape the buzzes emanating from the ether – the dots and dashes heard by the interceptor. Then the length of the dashes was measured by running the tape through another machine. In this way the identity of the sender could be assessed scientifically.

Y service personnel were not just responsible for tracking the senders on important networks but also provided vital information for the codebreakers. As already shown, the metadata contained in the preamble of signals was almost as important as the content of the messages, as was the radio-operators' chatter. Knowing who the sender was, where the sender was and what was going on – all information which might be indiscreetly imparted in the chatter – could provide vital information helping the Bletchley Park codebreakers put together a crib.

In time the interception operation grew, in proportion as the value which Enigma decrypts contributed to the overall intelligence picture. German Air Force and Army Enigma provided the most food for the Bombes, and in time the army Y service, under the War Office Y Group, came to represent three-quarters of the army intercept operation. Fifty new women operators were arriving at Chicksands each month in 1943, and Chicksands was producing one million 'groups' – in the case of Enigma messages, a 'group' consisted of five morse code letters – of intercept every week by February that year. Those groups had to get to Bletchley from the interception sites. Y stations were located all over the British Isles and beyond; the strain on the telecommunications infrastructure continued to be a problem throughout the war, with some messages having to go to Bletchley on the back of a motorbike even during 1944 – but as Bletchley was only 30 minutes' ride away from Chicksands, so this solution was at least workable for them.

Motorcycle despatch riders would rush signals forms to Bletchley, arriving in the stable yard. But motorcycle transport was slow and unreliable – sending the intercepts via a landline was faster and safer. In February 1943, Block E – one of the new, ugly, brick and steel wartime constructions on the Bletchley Park site – was completed

A 'W/T Red' form on which Y service listeners wrote down the 5-letter groups of morse code letters they heard.

and became the Bletchley Park Communications Centre, complete with a 'teleprinter annex' – a vast hall, now housing a D-Day exhibit as part of the Bletchley Park Trust's museum. Teleprinters chattered away day and night, spewing out the intercepted signals, and, vitally, sending off the intelligence results when the decryption processes had been completed.

The Y service in numbers

September 1939: 19 Army interception wireless sets in operation

September 1941: 132 interception sets in use for Enigma, with 35 each at Beaumanor and Chicksands, 21 at Harpenden, 14 at Sandridge and 10 at Aldershot, with the others in various locations

October 1941: Chicksands has 50 sets deployed on Enigma, spread between keys thus: Red, 24; Light Blue, 7; Mustard, 3; Brown, 1; Chaffinch, 1; and with 14 used on 'search' (finding wavelengths on which transmissions were being broadcast)

November 1941: 76 Army interception wireless sets in operation; but Commander Travis of Bletchley says 300 sets are required for Enigma traffic

October 1943: War Office Y station at Kedleston Hall newly in operation with 36 sets; Beaumanor (including its outstation at Bishop's Waltham) has 150 operational sets

November 1943: 135 receivers in operation at Chicksands devoted to Enigma, with 14 sets devoted to other types of signal

May 1944: Teleprinter lines into Bletchley Park: from Beaumanor, 22; from Chicksands, 21; from Forest Moor, 18; from Kedleston 6; and from Shenley, 4

The first thing to be done when raw intercepts arrived at Bletchley was to sort and register them. It might sound dull, but with many thousands of intercepts arriving every day, order and system was vital. Plus, the very process of organizing and cataloguing the different types of message could yield up helpful information of use to the codebreakers. At its simplest, the initial ground-setting for the three Enigma rotors in German Army and air force traffic, supposedly chosen at random, might be a complete giveaway to the secret message setting: the bored Enigma operator might choose **HIT** as the 'random' ground-setting, which made the sequence **LER** an odds-on favourite for the message setting, potentially saving hours of Bombe time and giving away a big part of the key of the day. Another example comes from the key used by the SS to send in routine returns from concentration camps, enumerating the number of detainees transferred in, out or died. These grim numbers were encoded using letters to replace numbers. The code changed daily – and the cryptanalysts learned that the pattern followed exactly the plugboard pairings, so that this most difficult part of the Enigma puzzle was handed to the codebreakers on a plate.

Sorting out the incoming traffic according to the 'key' used for the different messages was of first importance. Each network and military specialism had its own key-sheets defining the Enigma settings to be used each day: all messages sent with the same 'key' would share the same plugboard cross-pluggings, the same rotor choice and order, and the same ring-settings on the rotors, with only the message-specific ground and message settings differing from one signal to another. There were dozens of different keys; to begin with, the traffic analysts working with Welchman at the Elmers School segregated messages in different keys using coloured pencils. The number of keys in use rapidly exceeded the variety of colours on offer, so birds came to be used as well. Naval keys tended to be named after sea-creatures (Dolphin, Shark, Porpoise), but on the whole keys named after fish were reserved for non-Enigma teleprinter ciphers. When bird-life ran short, other keys were named after insects, animals, vegetables and flowers. The most important key, throughout the war, was the 'Red' key, used by the German Air Force but – owing to the close liaison between ground and air forces for German attack tactics – of considerable value to the ground-based armed forces as well.

A selection of Enigma keys	
Red	German Air Force key, continually broken from autumn 1940 onwards
Yellow	German Norway campaign key
Brown	German Air Force key used in connection with navigational beams, directing bombers to British targets
Orange	SS key
Cockroach	12th Air Corps key, important because of the operational area of the corps directly across the Channel
Vulture	Panzer army key, Eastern Front
Kestrel	German Army-Air Force liaison key
Chaffinch	Rommel's Africa Corps key used in Libya
Raven	German Army key used in the Balkans
Primrose	German Air Force administration key used in North Africa
Beetle	German Air Force command, Eastern Front
Squirrel	Long-range bomber key used in Italy
Weasel	Anti-aircraft units in Russia

After registration, a day's Enigma messages were passed to the cryptanalysts in Hut 6 (or, for Naval Enigma, Hut 8) to devise menus for connecting up the wiring on the Bombes. The process was to begin with a likely word or phrase, match it against the intercept in such a way as to avoid a position where a letter would encipher as itself, and build a 'menu' or wiring diagram containing as many loops as possible. Creating a menu from a good crib was an art form.

The process was not straightforward. To begin with, messages might be garbled or groups could be missing. The Enigma operator at the German end might have made a mistake. Although the elementary errors made by German signals staff in choosing settings can be laughed at, in other respects German signals discipline was not just good but sophisticated. Abbreviations, codenames and jargon all made the task of cribbing hard. Especially after the Battle of El Alamein in 1942 there were clever efforts to improve security: adding nonsense (called 'Quatsch') sequences at the beginning or end of messages, to conceal stereotyped salutations; burying signatures in the middle of the message; and adding dummy letters. Use of the 'discriminant' – part of the preamble which told the receiving station which key was being used for the message – was changed in 1943 and even dropped altogether on some army and air force keys. All these things caused difficulties for the codebreakers.

Still, military organizations like order and standardization, so once the system was understood, cribs might be easier to find. Sometimes it was easy, because units would encipher such non-secret phrases as 'Nothing to report' or 'Weather report'. But even when the signallers were more subtle a way in might be found. Communications between Berlin and North Africa might contain a phrase such as **IDA DACHS AN OTTO TAUBE** – meaningless, apparently, except to the initiated, who understood 'Ida Dachs' to be a code-name for the Chief of Army Signals in Berlin and 'Otto Taube' to be the Senior Signals Officer for the Panzer Army in Africa. If the crib-maker knew the identity of the signaller and the type of network, this kind of address information could allow a crib to be created.

The Oxford mathematics graduate Ann Williamson found herself nominated to the 'Machine Room' in Hut 6 in 1943:

After two or three weeks in Hut 6 'school' I started in the MR (Machine Room) on three shifts 9 a.m. to 4 p.m., 4 to midnight and midnight to 9 a.m. with roughly two weeks on each. There were, I think, about a dozen of us on each shift, mostly with degrees in maths, economics or law. I believe that those subjects were thought to lead to meticulousness and accuracy. The MR was connected by a door and a hatch to Hut 6 Watch which was the vital hub around which the whole hut worked. The Machine Room was so called because it had a number of Enigma machines....

Teleprinter messages encoded by the Germans on their Enigma machines were received and listed in the two RRs (Registration Rooms) .... Members of the Watch decided which messages had been sent in which codes and what the original text probably was. They wrote out, by hand, some of the jumbled nonsense which had been received and underneath wrote the probable German text; the crib, which was essential to breaking any code.

Constructing a good crib was a difficult business. If the crib was too long, the chances were that a turnover of the middle rotor would occur somewhere along the sequence of letters making up the crib, which would ruin the consistency test on which the Bombe machines depended. On the other hand, if the crib was too short or contained too many repetitions of the same letter, there would be too few loops in the menu which would lead to a profusion of 'false stops'. Ann Williamson described the optimum menu design: links between six pairs of letters with four 'closures' or loops (a '6 and 4' menu), or 9 and 3, 12 and 2 or 15 and 1. 'The more compact the better.'

Ann Williamson of the Machine Room

Ann Williamson worked in Hut 6 at Bletchley Park as a Temporary Assistant. That job title probably conjures up a picture of clerical drudgery typical of the experience of many young women at Bletchley during the war years.

The truth was a little different. Job descriptions followed conventional gender patterns for the 1940s, where men were paid more than women, and certain highly-paid roles could only be done by men. Even at GC&CS the titles were misleading, with the word 'assistant' typically meaning codebreaker. Ann Williamson was a mathematics graduate from Oxford who worked in the Machine Room. The Machine Room didn't house a Bombe, but it had originally contained a rare example of a reconstructed Enigma machine for the codebreakers to work with. To confuse things even more thoroughly, by the time she joined Hut 6, the Machine Room was located in Block D, though the activity of the team still went under the name 'Hut 6'.

Miss Williamson's role was to put together the menus for what she called the 'programming' of the Bombes. Later in the war she helped with 'dud-busting', which meant dealing with messages which didn't decipher properly, possibly because the sender's Enigma machine had been mis-set, or because of a corruption in transmission. Dud-busting was solving puzzles of a mathematical nature. She also helped out teaching mathematics to girl students working towards their School Certificate (nowadays replaced by the GCSE).

By the time she died in 2020 aged 97, Ann Mitchell (as she now was) had clocked up a formidable career which busted expectations about women's roles in the post-war years. In the 1950s she trained in marriage guidance, and her work led her to discover that nobody had researched the effects of divorce on children. Taking up the subject for herself, she researched and wrote books on the subject and achieved changes to the law in Scotland to ensure children's needs had to be taken into account in divorce settlements.

Menus were sent off to be turned into wiring patterns for the cables at the rear of the Bombes. Even this was not such a straightforward process: Bombe time was at a premium, and although the supply of Bombes accelerated during the war there was always a need for coordination and prioritization. Rising from small beginnings (two Bombes at Bletchley Park in late 1940) to a peak of over 200 Bombes in early 1945, it was never feasible to have Bletchley Park itself act as the home for all Bombe activity. For one thing, it would be unwise to have all the cryptanalytical machinery on a single site. In 1941, local manor houses were pressed into service, with houses at Adstock, Gayhurst and Wavendon giving up part of their grounds to accommodate Bombes and their operators. But all these places were limited in space even though they were local enough to be controlled from Bletchley. The success of the offensive against Enigma meant that a much larger, radically larger, deployment was needed.

In 1942 the decision was taken to build specific outstations devoted to Enigma codebreaking. At the end of the Bakerloo underground line, a suitable site was identified at Stanmore, where a building in the same style as the new brick-and-steel edifices going up at Bletchley itself was rapidly constructed. By the end of the year 16 Bombes were installed, growing to 75 Bombes by the end of hostilities. But the Stanmore outstation was not enough. An even larger facility began to be planned, also in the outskirts of London, this time at Eastcote. The first Bombes arrived there towards the end of 1943, and during the coming months the number would increase to more than 100. Eastcote was, in fact, so important as a location that, on the disbandment of Bletchley Park as the home of the GC&CS and its recreation as Government Communications Headquarters (GCHQ) once the war was over, it became the home of the whole GCHQ organization.

All these Bombes in all these places enhanced the need for careful control and coordination. In Hut 23 at Bletchley – a temporary wooden building which had once been numbered Hut 3, but once the Enigma operation named 'Hut 3' had migrated to one of the more solid brick blocks, thus becoming 'Hut 3 in Block D' after February 1943 – was the Control Room. On a wall of the Control Room werc panels showing each of the different Bombes available for operation. They were grouped according to the bays in which the Bombes were located, with the bays named after allied combatant countries and the Bombes after cities in those countries. Bombes shut down for maintenance or repair were labelled 'U/S' for 'unserviceable', and menus were assigned to the others. A bank of telephones provided communication between the outstations and Bletchley, and allowed the results of apparently valid stops to be phoned back to the Control Room.

> The head of shift in the MR kept a list of which menu was put on which bombes and at what time... [A] STOP would be phoned to and recorded by the MR, and one of us would immediately set up an Enigma machine with that wheel order and with the plugs in ... We'd then turn the wheels to show AAA and use the keyboard like a typewriter, first to confirm that the links in the STOP fitted the menu, by typing the jumbled letters to see whether they gave the expected German text, and second to decode more of the text to see whether the rest of the crib decoded as it should... If successful, we'd call for a member of the Watch (who was possibly already breathing down our neck) and hope that he or she would call 'Red's up!'

Once the key was revealed, the way was open to deciphering proper. All the messages sent on a broken key could be deciphered by setting up an Enigma machine in exactly the same way that the intended German recipient would set up his own machine. Bletchley Park had only a very few Enigma machines: the first being the precious Polish gift of a reconstructed machine in 1939, others from occasional captures; there were certainly not enough Enigmas to enable the large-scale deciphering exercise implied by daily successes against prolific keys.

To address the Enigma machine shortage the deciphering clerks were equipped with Typex machines. Typex was a blatant copy of Scherbius's Enigma technology. It was Britain's own rotor-based cipher machine, with additional functionality such as simultaneous typing of the plain- and cipher-texts on to paper strips, and a plugboard facility. Although Typex was designed to have more rotors than Enigma, it could be made to work like an Enigma with specially wired rotors replicating the behaviour of Enigma rotors, and dummies which made no actual change to the encipherment in the extra slots. Enciphered intercepts were handed to Typex operators who set up their machines as instructed in each message's preamble, and then typed in the jumble of ciphertext to give out the plaintext on one of the Typex's thin paper tapes. The paper strips were then pasted onto larger paper sheets, leaving plenty of space for 'emendation' – that is, the correction of misspellings, garbles and other errors – from where they could be given to linguist-intelligence officers for translation (a non-trivial process where military jargon is concerned) and evaluation.

Not every translated message had equivalent value. Signals which were prized by the codebreakers because they contained ideas for cribs might be worthless to commanders in the field. Signals which contained snippets of organizational information could be of intelligence value only when combined with other knowledge. An assessment system, based around the needs of the intelligence functions of the armed forces, was essential, although to begin with not everyone was happy about it. 'The enigma results are of an order of certainty differing wholly from the products of most other intelligence sections... I have no intention of continuing to work as an obscure subsidiary of Commander Clarke.' This was Dilly Knox, grumbling in 1940 that the product of his 'Research Section' had to go through the Naval Section, then led by W.F. Clarke – perhaps one of the few veteran codebreakers of Knox's era who could match Knox for cantankerousness. Knox lost this battle, though it took another year or two before a completely satisfactory way of dovetailing cryptanalysis with intelligence evaluation was worked out.

Meanwhile, the minutiae of message content were collected, regardless of their immediate appeal to battlefield tacticians. One of Bletchley Park's triumphs was the creation of a complex cross-referencing system, largely based on the meticulous recording of small items of data found in the content of deciphered messages on to ordinary cardboard filing cards. Information about even junior officers in the German Army might be of interest when associated with other data.

One instance arose in May 1941, after the Battle of the Denmark Strait when the German battleship *Bismarck* sank HMS *Hood* with tragic loss of life. The reputation of the Royal Navy was at stake after this fateful encounter, with all efforts trained on locating the *Bismarck* and bringing her to account. Except that *Bismarck* had disappeared into the grey wastes of the Atlantic, out of sight and out of radar contact, heading for an unknown destination. There were various theories; one was that *Bismarck* might return to a German-controlled port on the west coast of France, but there was no solid evidence supporting any of the theories. But then – from German Air Force Enigma – came a message from air force General Hans Jeschonnek, who was then in Athens in connection with the invasion of Crete, concerned about a relative serving on *Bismarck*. The message was sent in the Red Enigma key, and the information gleaned enabled the codebreakers to deduce that *Bismarck* was proceeding to Brest. The

Royal Navy could now close in, and the fate of *Hood* became the fate of *Bismarck*.

To enable messages of pressing importance to be prioritized, the intelligence assessors at Bletchley graded deciphered signals with a number of Zs, ranging from Z (lowest) to ZZZZZ (highest). Decrypts would be accompanied by commentary, carefully segregated from the decrypted text, which would enable the reader to understand the sometimes arcane jargon used in the original, to remind the reader of the significance of the personnel, places or units referred to in the signal, or to join the dots to other signals which together made up an intelligence picture. Sometimes the messages would go direct to a theatre of operations; others simply went to the ministry in London. Prime Minister Winston Churchill had a personal fondness for decrypts, asking for the juiciest ones to be delivered to him personally in a locked box, all the better to berate his military commanders when he considered they were falling short on the aggressive war he wished to sustain.

Providing Enigma intelligence to commanders, or even to White-hall officials, generated its own collection of problems. Everyone from Churchill downwards accepted, in principle at least, the notion that the 'source' should be protected – in other words that the enemy should never get the slightest hint that the Enigma was compromised. For, if that were known, the system would be changed, and the way into any replacement system was likely to be a long, hard road constituting an almost complete intelligence blackout. Secrecy was all, but a source which cannot be used is a useless source. A secure, useable system for exploitation was needed.

The first English writer to bring the secret of Enigma codebreaking to light was Group Captain Frederick Winterbotham, whose connection to Bletchley was that of an intelligence officer rather than codebreaker. His book is open to criticism on a number of counts, but

Winterbotham is on surer ground when he describes the system set up to bring cryptanalytical intelligence into the hands of commanders. His scheme was to establish 'Special Liaison Units' (SLUs), located with commanders' intelligence teams, which (unlike the majority of field officers) were in on the secret. The SLUs were to receive the information in secure form, enciphered either with a one-time pad or the Typex machine (which, it was hoped, the Germans could not break).

To make the system work it would be slow and inefficient to rely on the telephone or motorcycle couriers to get the gems out of Bletchley Park. Fortunately, Bletchley Park's proximity to the main telecommunications link between London and the industrial north came to its aid: it was relatively straightforward to connect Bletchley with a secure cable, and messages went direct to the chiefs of staff and their own assessors – and in printed form, the juicy ones could still go to Churchill in his locked box.

Apart from communications, the system strictly limited the personnel allowed to know about and see 'Ultra', the codeword given to intelligence derived from decrypts. Security began at home – with the Bletchley Park organization initially struggling to modernize its approach to physical security as well as the need-to-know system. Famously, all new staff were expected to sign the Official Secrets Act form warning them of dire consequences of disclosing what they knew. It had not always been as professional as that: a memo of 6 April 1940 has Alastair Denniston setting out a procedure for personnel entering the Park after 7 pm:

1st Challenge.   Halt! who goes there (in loud voice).
                         Answer: Friend.
                         If individual or group of persons halt they will be told to advance friend and be

recognised and then asked to give the pass word. If they cannot give the pass word, they will be conducted to the watchman for recognition.

If they fail to halt:-

2nd Challenge.   Halt or I fire.

Security at Bletchley itself, however, was not the real concern, even though there was the odd scare. In 1941 the detective-story writer Agatha Christie caused a minor stir because she named a character in one of her books – a character who knows Britain's wartime secrets – 'Major Bletchley'. Miss Christie happened to be a friend of Dilly Knox, and the authorities feared the worst. It all turned out to be a horrible coincidence, with the Major taking the name Bletchley only because Miss Christie had been delayed at Bletchley on a train journey and taken a dislike to the place.

More significant was the questions of how the intelligence could reach its destination safely, and how it could be put to good yet prudent use. Often the recipient of the intelligence conveyed by the decrypts would not have been indoctrinated, giving the SLU team a tricky task of balancing their knowledge of the information's reliability against the innate scepticism of those who could not know why the source was so highly trusted. All sorts of disguises and ruses were used. The thin disguise might be constructed as 'Following report, seen in the files of the German Army in Tunisia on 6/4/43', or 'Source saw on 18/11 an order', with garbles and missing groups explained as 'Source saw incompletely burned document'. The security afforded by this was probably illusory, since the verbatim copying of original decrypts was what investigators on both sides used to check up on their own cipher security. Keeping the paperwork out of enemy hands, and limiting the flow of paperwork, were much more important. Once read, messages were to be destroyed.

A memo from Winterbotham written in December 1942 gives a sense of the difficulties:

1. The plans and operations of the Tunisia campaign are being based largely on ULTRA information.

2. This information is being properly digested by an experienced Intelligence officer from Bletchley Park before being submitted to the Commanders.

3. All Commanders who receive and use this information have now been personally visited, the security at each Command has been checked, special communications to each Command laid on, and advice as to how to use ULTRA securely, given...

5. The presence of an officer with full experience of the distribution and security of ULTRA, and full powers to undertake the duties now accomplished and set out in paragraph 3, is vitally necessary. This officer should accompany the Command of any future operation since the early stages of an operation are the most vulnerable as regards security.

Further rules on use of 'Ultra' precluded indoctrinated officers being placed in combat zones where they were at personal risk of capture; and the careful use of cover when 'Ultra' was used as the basis for an operation. When the Enigma messages decrypted by Knox's team at Bletchley laid the foundation for the attack on the Italian fleet at Matapan, the source was protected by having a spotter plane fly over the fleet – the point being that the spotter plane was not so much to spot the fleet, but be spotted by it.

A vehicle adapted for SLU reception, in the North African campaign.

Commanding officers did not always respect the rules. Winterbotham records

> I had to tell them at one and the same time that they would be supplied with the actual signals of the enemy on the highest level, and that they must also conform to strict security regulations as to its use, the main one being that they must not take any immediate action on the information which might lead the enemy to suspect that we knew his plans... Some commanders were ... a bit unhappy about the restrictions put on its use.

Aggressive in-the-know generals refused to stay in safe quarters far from the front: US Generals Patton and Doolittle took risks but without ill effect. Sometimes the information was too tempting to resist, as when the US Navy targeted refuelling 'milch cow' submarines in 1944, causing the Germans to put in place a new investigation into the security of their own communications.

That, however, is to anticipate success on Naval Enigma, which in the early years of World War II remained elusive. The Naval Enigma was more resistant to attack than German Army and Air Force Enigma. Notwithstanding that the greatest threat to the survival of Britain came from the sea, the ease with which army and air force intelligence could be squeezed from Enigma directed resources away from the intractable naval problem into these more profitable areas. Huts 4 and 8 were likely to dry up unless something could be done. But the head of Hut 8 was Alan Turing. Maybe something was possible.

CHAPTER SIX

The Naval Enigma

The German Navy's approach to Enigma differed in small but significant particulars from that of the German Army and air force. At the start of the war, they added a further three rotors to the five already available: not only did this increase the number of rotor permutations available on any given day to 336, compared with the 60 which had already given the Poles such difficulties in early 1939, but the wirings of the three new rotors needed to be found.

Bletchley Park's Enigma team knew all about finding wiring in new rotors, but their techniques depended on having, ideally, a crib of 26 letters and a 'depth of two' – meaning that two messages had been sent using the same setting. For Naval Enigma, that was a tall order, because the availability of cribs depended on knowing what the naval units were saying to each other. Naval jargon, and the basic everyday content of naval messages, comes from a wholly different dictionary from that of other armed forces.

Worse, the German Navy had seen the flaws in the army-air force approach to 'indicators' (the start-of-message information which told the recipient how to orientate the Enigma rotors for the beginning of decipherment). In May 1937 a far more secure method was adopted, relying on a *Kenngruppenbuch*, or K-book, in which three-letter sequences for message settings were printed out. To disguise the sequences in radio transmissions, a bigram substitution cipher was used. Alan Turing explained the system in his 144-page typescript on Enigma codebreaking, which he wrote in about 1941 and became known as 'Prof's book', since Alan Turing was nicknamed 'Prof' by other codebreakers at Bletchley.

> To encipher a message the operator chooses two trigrammes out of a book. The first of these trigrammes is called the 'Schluesselkenngruppe' .... The second trigramme is called the Verfahrenkenngruppe.

The *Verfahrenkenngruppe* trigram was the message setting – the three letters which the operator needed to have showing through the viewing windows of his Enigma machine at the start of encipherment or decipherment. The *Schlüsselkenngruppe* was an additional sequence intended to hide the *Verfahrenkenngruppe*. Alan Turing goes on:

> Suppose the Schluesselkenngruppe is CIV and the Verfahrenkenngruppe is TOD, then the operator chooses two dummy letters, Q and X say, and writes this down

> Q C I V
> T O D X

... From the eight letters above, one also obtains the indicator for the message, by substitution from a table which gives bigramme for bigramme. The substitution is done by replacing the vertical pairs above the bigrammes, e.g. in this case, if the substitute for QT were DA, and TH for CO, PO for ID, and CN for VX then the indicator for the message is DATH POCN. Apart from the Schluessselkenngruppe feature this is the method we had inferred was being used.

When the receiver of the message got **DATH POCN**, he reversed the process: he looked up the bigrams **DA**, **TH**, **PO** and **CN** in his book, lined them up in a rectangle, and used only the first three letters of the second line in the grid as his message setting. It was complex but it was very secure.

In the last sentence quoted above, Alan Turing was being slightly coy. Once the Bombe machine concept had been handed over to the British Tabulating Machine company for design and development, he had not been entirely idle. The challenge of Naval Enigma was reportedly assigned to him, partly because it was so difficult that he found it interesting, and partly because nobody else was working on it – all of which suited him grandly. By studying the patterns of indicators actually used in German Naval Enigma traffic, Turing had actually uncovered the system (apart, as he says, from the *Schlüsselkenngruppe* feature; but as this was the part of the key discarded by the receiver, it was hardly a big omission).

Unfortunately, the breakthrough in understanding the indicator process did not bring the Bletchley Park naval team any closer to reading any German Enigma messages. The problem was the secret bigram tables – the substitution charts which showed that **QT** was converted to **DA** and so forth. Unless the codebreakers could get hold of one of these, they would have to use far more tedious methods of searching for the daily key and the message settings in use.

With the benefit of Alan Turing's insight, and a timely interrogation of a captured German Navy radio operator, two new lines of attack were devised. The prisoner of war had revealed – without knowing it was a secret – that the Germans had changed the method of transmitting numbers in Enigma messages. The Enigma keyboard, unlike a computer or typewriter keyboard, had no numbers; the solution, to begin with, was to pretend that the top line of the keyboard was in fact numbers and to indicate the switch to figures with the character **Y**. To give an example, the second part of a two-part message might begin with the sequence (before encipherment) **FORTYWEEPYYWEEPY**, where **FORT** meant 'continuation' and **WEEP** meant '2330', or 'continuation of message 2330 repeat 2330'. It was the Polish codebreakers who spotted this particular example, giving the name FortyWeepy to one of the more obscure and lesser-known techniques of codebreaking. But in 1937 FortyWeepy ceased to work. The new method of transmitting numbers, as revealed by the prisoner, was to type the numbers in full.

It was tedious and slow for the Enigma operators, but a gift, of sorts, to the codebreakers in Hut 8. Messages beginning **FORT** seemed to be amenable to cribbing if the German words **EINS, ZWO** (telegraphese for *zwei*) or **DREI** were tried. In fact, around 90 per cent of messages actually contained the word **EINS** somewhere in them. Resigned codebreakers compiled, by hand, a full catalogue of all 17,000 ways in which the word **EINS** could be enciphered with a given key on any given day. Then the messages of the day were scrutinized for these four-letter sequences – giving a clue to the possible daily set-up of the Enigma. The amounts of concentration required and tedium endured beggar belief. But according to the *History of Hut Eight*, written in 1945 by one of its members, A.P. Mahon, about one hit in four was a correct guess at the set-up, 'so that messages were broken fairly rapidly.' Mahon goes on to say that punched-card Hollerith machinery took over the process later in the war, no doubt to the great relief of the staff in Hut 8.

The other technique, derived from a method for identifying the fast-moving right-hand rotor conceived by Jerzy Różycki, was called 'Banburismus'. Różycki's approach was based on the principle that, if the same substitution cipher is used to transform two different messages, the frequency-count of letters mirrors the frequency with which letters appear in plain language.

Frequency counts and depths

Scrabble-players are highly attuned to the relative frequency with which letters occur in the English language: letters like E, T and N, which occur all the time, score one point, while rarer ones like X and J score 8 and the almost-never-seen Q and Z score 10. Where a substitution cipher has been used, where each letter in the cipher corresponds to a single letter in the unchanged alphabet, it is a simple matter to count up the number of times each letter occurs in a piece of enciphered text to work out what the cipher is. This is not a curiosity of English: a German-language frequency table might look like this:

Letter	Relative Frequency
E	16.93 per cent
N	10.53 per cent
I	8.02 per cent
R	6.89 per cent
...	...
Q	0.02 per cent

(These figures are for standard modern German. The version of German used for Enigma messages was peppered with jargon and unorthodox spelling conventions, so the frequency counts would have been slightly different. But the basic idea is the same.)

If a more sophisticated cipher system, such as Enigma, is used, the cipher disguises the frequency count of the original message, so that the cipher-text has a near random (3.85 per cent) distribution of letters.

One result of the non-random distribution of letters in plain language can be seen if two samples of text are lined up one beneath the other. Because 'E's will occur much more often than other letters, there's a good chance that 'E's will be one above the other more than $\frac{1}{26}$ of the time, and the same is true for other letters. In fact, with German text, one should expect a coincidence about $\frac{1}{17}$ (5.9 per cent) of the time.

A very useful piece of knowledge is that the same result happens if the same settings were used to encipher two different messages on an Enigma machine. If the left and middle rotors do not move, the substitution alphabets will be identical between the two messages for any text as the right-hand rotor cycles through from a given starting-point. In such a case, two different messages could be written out, one under the other, and the coincidences counted – if it's one in seventeen, or thereabouts, that implies a 'depth'. This change in probabilities was the foundation of the 'Banburismus' technique, and it meant that Bletchley Park's codebreakers used up an awful lot of squared paper.

Banburismus was invented by Alan Turing shortly after he had solved the structure of the German Naval Enigma indicator. Intercepted messages were transcribed on to long sheets of paper in which the (regular) alphabet had been printed in vertical lines; these sheets were printed in the town of Banbury, giving rise to the name of the technique. Each vertical line of letters gave the 26 possibilities for a given letter in the intercept. Transcription was done by punching a hole through the relevant letter. Then the sheets were placed on top of each other and slid sideways, first to identify higher-than-random coincidences, and then to look for strings of adjacent coincidences. Lots of coincidences implied a common rotor set-up.

When the codebreakers knew that the starting rotor positions for different messages were identical, except for the right-hand rotor, they could tease out information about the alphabetical substitution being made by the Enigma rotors by linking the depths they had identified. For example:

- Imagine that Banbury sheets show a lot of coincidences between two messages, for which the rotor start positions shown by the indicator were **WDV** and **WDA**. This implies that the rotor set-up was identical for both messages, except that the right-hand Enigma rotor was five positions further on at the start of enciphering the second message. But the highest number of coincidences was found, in this case, not where the sheets are offset by five places, but eight. The codebreakers could express this mathematically as '**V = A +** 8'; they ignored the first two letters of the indicator in these equations.
- Then they could look for other pairs of messages where there were high levels of coincidence when only the third letter of the indicator differed, and make similar equations, like '**X =** **B** + 3', '**B = H +** 2' and '**H = V** – 4'. The equations spelt out the separation of the letters in the substitution alphabet carried out by the Enigma machine, and could be strung together in chains (in this case, **A - - - - H - B - VX**).
- The chain could then be checked against a true A to Z

alphabet found on the rim of an Enigma rotor, to ensure that there were no crashes – that is to say, letters enciphering as themselves, in the same way that a ciphertext is checked against a crib. When a good position was found, that might give a clue to the turnover position of the right-hand rotor, which must be outside the limits of the chain. In this example, the chain matches the alphabet with a turnover implied somewhere after the letter 'D', which might suggest that the moving rotor is Rotor II, which has its turnover notch between 'E' and 'F'.

Chain	A					H		B		V	X
Alphabet	T	U	V	W	X	Y	Z	A	B	C	D

As A. P. Mahon remarked, 'This ... shows clearly the fallacy of the system of having all the wheels [rotors] turning over in different places. It was this characteristic alone which made it possible to distinguish the wheels by Banburismus and reduce the number of wheel orders to be tried. Wheels 6, 7 and 8 [the three extra rotors specific to the German Navy] were indistinguishable from one another and a great nuisance to the Banburist.'

Later in the war some of the tedious sorting work was taken over by punched-card processes on Hollerith machines; Banburismus was destined to be a major source of attack on Naval Enigma for over two years, but not until the spring of 1941. In the meantime, there was a problem. Banburismus was doomed unless the bigram tables which disclosed the indicator were known.

As Hugh Alexander, Alan Turing's deputy in (and later head of) Hut 8 explained:

Turing was now faced with the following dilemma. There were

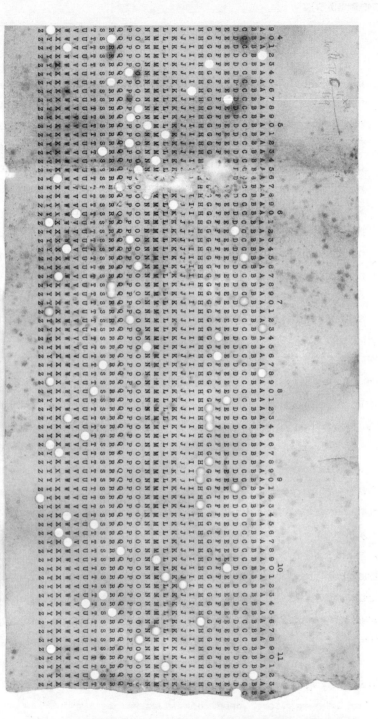

A Banbury sheet found during renovations at Bletchley Park.

only two ways of getting into a key (1) Cribbing (2) Banburismus. Cribbing required some detailed knowledge of the traffic since otherwise one could not predict what a message would say; it therefore seemed necessary to break a few days on Banburismus first. Banburismus needed no knowledge of the content of the traffic but needed at least one known bigram table; it therefore seemed necessary to break a few days on Cribbing first. A further difficulty was that the bombes – essential to complete the break on modern keys – did not start to arrive until the Summer of 1940 and the German Air and Army section working on Enigma (Hut 6) also needed these machines. Thus the testing of even one crib, supposing this to be available, presented a considerable problem.

Joan Clarke

Joan Clarke was an undergraduate studying mathematics at Newnham College, Cambridge, when she was approached by her supervisor in geometry with a strange proposition. There was some war work which might suit her: it 'did not really need mathematics but mathematicians tended to be good at it.' The supervisor was Gordon Welchman. Joan accepted, and on completing Part III of her mathematics course – the supplementary year equivalent to a Master's degree, not that Cambridge gave degrees to women then – she joined Bletchley Park in Hut 8 under Alan Turing.

Joan's background gives few clues to how she came to be at Cambridge studying mathematics at such an elevated level. Her father was a vicar and her grandfather an archbishop. Her brother Martin was an academic, certainly, a fellow at King's College, Cambridge, and a near-contemporary of Alan Turing there; Martin was a classicist. To study, and a non-arts subject at that, was a relatively unconventional path for a young woman in the inter-war years, but Joan's choices had been supported by her family.

At Bletchley she quickly established a reputation as one of the foremost codebreakers. She excelled at 'Banburismus', a process which required an unusual combination of patience, attention to detail, analysis of probabilities, and insight. Not many people were very good at Banburismus, because it is painstaking and often very unrewarding. But in fact Joan was so good, not just at this technique but more generally, that she had to be promoted. This, of course, was impossible, because the two codebreaker grades in the service were men's roles, and Joan was a woman.

The solution was to make her a linguist. She filled in the application form: 'I enjoyed answering a questionnaire with "grade linguist, languages none".' Later promotions were more difficult, and Joan later wrote with some wry acidity about pay grades and gender. 'There was a move to increase the pay of those who had qualifications which were not relevant, which I knew about through hearing some of the girls discussing whether one of them might benefit as a trained hairdresser.'

Nevertheless, her skills were recognized, and when the vast majority of Bletchley Park's staff were demobilized at the end of the war Joan stayed on at the newly re-named GCHQ, where she remained until the organization moved to Cheltenham in 1952. That was an important year: she married fellow GCHQ employee Jock Murray – and they moved to Crail, in Fifeshire. They were much too young to 'retire', there was no obvious reason to move to Scotland, and it is an enduring mystery what occupied the Murrays while they were there, one only partly explained by a developing enthusiasm for solving historical puzzles relating to Reformation-era Scottish coinage, which required the same skills as Banburismus. Joan wrote several papers on this and similar topics, yet the sense remains that something doesn't quite add up. There are suggestions that there are local secret intelligence facilities near Crail which may have employed one or both of the Murrays. The mystery is compounded, since in 1962 Joan and Jock rejoined GCHQ.

Both remained there until retirement, in Joan's case well beyond the official retirement age.

Joan survived Jock, and died in 1996 aged 79. Joan Clarke was one of Bletchley's pre-eminent codebreakers, and one of the first to hammer on the glass ceiling of a male-dominated establishment (GCHQ has never had a woman Director). Unfortunately, Joan Clarke is more frequently remembered on account of her short engagement to Alan Turing. Even GCHQ's website gives this fact equal prominence to her work on Banburismus; she deserves better recognition, and in her own right.

There was, in fact, a method of recovering the bigram tables, using the catalogues of **EINS** encipherments, and a huge amount of labour. Put simply, the codebreakers were stumped, since they lacked the resources – people, or machinery, or both – to give effect to their good ideas. The only alternative was to hope for some good luck.

On 12 February 1940 the minesweeper HMS *Gleaner* was proceeding in the Firth of Clyde, when a U-boat was detected. A depth charge attack was instigated, which, in the shallow coastal waters, could have only one result. The unfortunate prey was *U-33*, which was on her third war patrol attempting to lay mines in the seaway leading to the important ports of the Clyde. The captain blew the tanks for emergency re-surfacing, but it was too late for most of the crew, 25 of whom perished with their boat. Among security precautions taken to protect the secrecy of Enigma, the captain had distributed rotors from the boat's Enigma machine among the crew, with instructions to jettison them once clear of the boat. The problem, for the captain, was that anything left on board in those shallow seas could readily be salvaged. So, regrettably, could anything found in the pockets of prisoners of war, and the carriers of rotors were captured and frisked before they could carry out their orders. Bletchley Park had its first stroke of luck: the rotors captured included two of the three with the previously unknown wiring which had been created specifically for the German Navy at the beginning of the war.

The next stroke of luck came during the otherwise ill-fated Norway campaign a couple of months later. A small (364 registered tons) German ship called, variously, *Julius Pickenpack*, *Polares* and *Schiff 26*, had been refitted as a supply ship for U-boats. *Schiff 26* was proceeding under a false Dutch flag off Moldefjord in company with another supply ship called *Schiff 37* when they were surprised by an overwhelmingly superior Royal Navy force comprising a heavy cruiser, two light cruisers and three destroyers. After *Schiff 37* had been sent to the bottom, the destroyers were sent off in pursuit of *Schiff 26*. HMS *Griffin* captured her and put a boarding party aboard to see what they could 'pinch'. The 'confidential books' had not been destroyed, and were swiftly sent off to Bletchley.

The *Schiff 26* haul validated the theoretical work of Alan Turing on the indicator system and provided enough material to enable German Naval Enigma to be read for a few remaining days in April 1940. But the materials were soon out of date. Likewise, when *U-13* was sunk near Lowestoft at the end of May, diving crews were sent down to retrieve what they could, but no helpful cipher material could be recovered. Part of the problem for salvage operations was that the Germans cannily printed the secret materials on soft paper in water-soluble ink. This didn't stop German Naval Intelligence launching an enquiry into the ongoing security of Enigma following the incident.

As A.P. Mahon recorded, the six months following the *Schiff 26* 'pinch' 'produced depressingly few results'. Frank Birch, overall head of the Naval Section at Bletchley Park, wrote to Commander Travis, 'I'm worried about Naval Enigma... Turing and Twinn are like people waiting for a miracle, without believing in miracles.' The miracle, if it were to materialize, would require imagination, theatre and a little human help. Fortunately, help was at hand.

During the inter-war period Frank Birch had developed a talent for acting and producing theatrical productions. He is often cited in the literature about Bletchley Park as having appeared as the Widow Twankey in *Aladdin*, but his talents went wider and deeper than the off-colour jokes in Christmas pantomimes. Birch had a fellow conspirator and scriptwriter in the Naval Intelligence Department called Ian Fleming, who was then serving as a Lieutenant Commander in the Royal Naval Volunteer Reserve before taking up the career for which he was later much better known, that of author of the James Bond novels. Between them, Birch and Fleming came up with a plot which was going to win World War II:

Operation Ruthless:
I suggest we obtain the loot by the following means
1. Obtain from Air Ministry an air-worthy German bomber (they have some).
2. Pick a tough crew of five, including a pilot, W/T operator and word perfect German speaker. Dress them in German Air Force uniform, add blood and bandages to suit.
3. Crash plane in Channel after making S.O.S. to rescue service in P/L [plain language].
4. Once aboard rescue boat, shoot German crew, dump overboard, bring rescue boat to English port.

A.P. Mahon comments drily that 'this somewhat ungentlemanly scheme was never put into practice.' Nevertheless, the fiction writers and producers were taken more seriously by those responsible for naval operations than one might expect. Things were getting worse, and some degree of ruthlessness was called for.

By the end of 1940 the Germans had shifted their strategy for cutting Britain's supply lifeline across the Atlantic. The emphasis, which had been on using the firepower of the German Navy's large capital ships and disguised raiders to attack merchant shipping, now moved to the expanding U-boat arm. Aided by the ability of Germany's own codebreakers to predict the sailing patterns of convoys, and the weak defences which the Royal Navy was provided as convoy escorts, U-boat commanders began to refer to the summer and autumn of 1940 as a 'happy time', since picking off merchant ships was so easy. By October 1940 they were sending 350,000 tons of merchant shipping to the bottom every month, and they were developing tactics which enabled them to surface in the middle of a convoy in the middle of the night and wreak utter havoc. By March 1941, 'the U-boat Command, its operational fleet about to enter at last upon a fairly rapid growth and its commanders prepared for the introduction of the new techniques of hunting and attacking the convoys in "wolf-packs", was embarking on the next stage of the Battle of the Atlantic with every expectation of achieving a decisive victory.'

Early in 1941 the planners of Royal Navy operations went on the offensive. Ostensibly the raid was about fish oil, but it would take a credulous audience to believe that fish oil was the commodity which would win or lose the war, even if glycerine is an important military by-product of the fish oil industry. But fish oil provided cover, and a story which could be told to the media, so the raid on the Lofoten Islands in early March 1941 known as Operation Claymore enabled a huge smokescreen to be created, quite literally, as the tanks of oil were burned down – while the more important, lower-key objectives of the raid could be carried out. The trawler *Krebs* which found herself in those northern waters was the target of another seizure and boarding-party, yielding the 'first important haul' of Enigma cipher documents for Bletchley Park. The haul enabled the whole of Naval Enigma to be

Troops return from the raid on the Lofoten Islands.

read for February 1941 – all out of date, and operationally useless, but from a cryptographic perspective of the greatest value in generating useable cribs.

The *Krebs* success pointed the way, and the Royal Navy looked for other targets. Sitting ducks are always good targets, and stationary warships constitute sitting ducks. Curiously, during this part of the war, the German Navy received its all-important weather reports – which enabled it to do its own forecasting – from weather ships on station in the far north of the Atlantic Ocean. The Royal Navy was not above seizing weather ships, and in May 1941 the *München* was captured, followed at the end of June by the *Lauenberg*, in both cases delivering up good 'pinches' for Bletchley Park. Added to these planned pinches there was the capture of *U-110* and her secret books in May; 'the crypt-analysts had derived so much information from these captures that Naval E [Enigma] was read for the rest of the war'.

That assessment, made by a Bletchley Park official after the event, was perhaps a little optimistic. In mid-1941 it still seemed an uphill struggle. The codebreakers were under-resourced and depending on pinches was inefficient and haphazard. They needed many more Bombe machines and far more staff. A few Wrens – women recruited into the Women's Royal Naval Service (WRNS) had arrived in March to operate Bombe machines and so free up codebreakers' time. But there were still only six Bombes at Bletchley in June, and priority was given to the straightforward, evidently successful army and air force versions of Enigma. Help, however, was available, if the codebreakers were willing to be sufficiently ruthless.

This time ruthlessness was not the work of Birch and Fleming, but that of Alan Turing and Gordon Welchman. Following a visit by the prime minister to congratulate his favourite spying group, the codebreakers of Bletchley Park, these two codebreakers, together with their respective Hut 8 and Hut 6 deputies, took the unthinkable step of writing direct to him to complain about their resourcing problems. All superior levels in the official chain of command were bypassed: Birch, Travis, Denniston, the head of MI6, you name it, all overtaken with a multi-page letter delivered by hand to Number 10 Downing Street. It's a miracle that the four authors didn't get fired. But perhaps this is because Travis (who is mentioned in glowing terms in the letter, and destined to take over the reins of command at Bletchley some months later) was let in on the conspiracy, or because under Denniston's weakening grip the management of Bletchley Park was already in question. Anyhow, the outcome, apart from the management shake-up, was that Churchill ordered 'Make sure they have everything they want, on extreme priority'. The block on resources was going to be lifted.

It might have been just in time, but the codebreakers had read enough Enigma messages to know that the run of success they were enjoying following the 1941 pinches was going to come to an abrupt end. The decodes revealed that the German Navy was going to change the U-boat Enigma system in a radical way, and that the change would take place early in 1942.

The 'M4' version of the Enigma machine raised its security by adding a fourth rotor. However, it was clever and versatile as well: the old turnaround wheel in the standard three-rotor machine was replaced by a new device doing the same job, called a 'thin reflector', and this made space for the fourth rotor. Two different thin reflectors were distributed, and two rotors for the fourth slot. These fourth-slot rotors were not interchangeable with the other rotors from the German Navy's set of eight: they were special rotors whose position was not 'stepped' by the movement of the other three, but could only be set to one of 26 positions during the set-up of the machine. Nevertheless, the extra features increased the number of different Enigma configurations from 150,000,000,000,000,000,000 to

60,000,000,000,000,000,000,000,000,000 – a 400,000-fold improvement in complexity, and a monstrous challenge for the codebreakers. The versatility of the machine was that it was reverse-compatible with the older versions of Enigma: with thin reflector 'b' and fourth rotor 'β', or with thin reflector 'c' and fourth rotor 'γ', and the fourth rotor in the **A** position, the machine would behave just like a standard three-rotor machine.

That versatility was, in the end, to be the undoing of the M4 Enigma. The versatility was needed for German weather reporting. Another improvement in German security was a switch to short-form reports, which cut the length of radio transmissions from ships and thus reduced the risk of the transmitting ship being located through radio direction-finding. The short signals for weather reporting were set out in a book and they were transmitted in a standardized order in the new M4 Enigma cipher. There were two flaws in the system: for weather reporting, the M4 was set up to behave like a three-rotor machine; and the weather reports once received by the German central meteorology station were re-coded and re-enciphered in a much simpler way, and broadcast more generally. The broadcasts were intercepted, decrypted at Bletchley, and furnished to Hut 8 as 'cribs' for the set-up of the Enigma machine. All that was needed was the codebook for the short weather code....

Bletchley Park had been given a copy of the old codebook which was in force until the beginning of 1942, the result of one of the 1941 pinches which had helped the Naval Section codebreakers so greatly during that year. But in January 1942 a new codebook came into force, followed the next month by the M4 version of Enigma, and a period of blackout descended during which Bletchley Park was unable to read Naval Enigma.

If it was a problem not having the short weather codebook, coping with the four-rotor M4 Enigma machine was a challenge of altogether enormous proportions. The sinkings by U-boats began inexorably to rise. The U-boats' successes were aided by the entry of the United States into the war at the beginning of December 1941 and the weak security precautions taken in respect of merchant shipping proceeding along the eastern seaboard of North America; but the inability of Bletchley to predict the movements of U-boats made the task of convoy escorts in the North Atlantic much more perilous. Something needed to be done, and the excuse that M4 was too big a problem was no excuse at all. It was self-evident that the Turing-Welchman Bombe machines designed for three-rotor Enigma were not going to be of any general use against the four-rotor M4, except in the case of the (now futile) short weather signals. A new approach was needed. To be exact, a new type of Bombe was needed.

A four-rotor Bombe was not going to be easy to build. The standard three-rotor machine was based around standard telephone-exchange electrical relays which allowed for the 17,576 possible positions of three Enigma rotors to be tested sequentially in around 12 minutes. Using the same kind of technology with an extra rotor to test implied a run-time of over five hours for each rotor order and each crib. It would slow down the decryption process to the point of unviability. If there was to be a four-rotor Bombe it would need a completely different engineering solution.

The prospect of an exciting new engineering project attracted bright sparks from all over, and the results of the consequent competition and backbiting were not wholly edifying. First of all, a partially electronic solution was put forward by the Telecommunications Research Establishment. This required long rotating shafts to be attached to a standard three-rotor Bombe with a thick snaking cable, a feature which meant that the adaptation soon became known as the 'cobra'. The shafts' function was to test the position of the fourth rotor and thus they had to revolve at very high speed, with the results recorded by the electronic unit which was the real innovation in this design. The mechanical part of the equipment was, however, at the limits of this older technology's accuracy; the electrical connections failed as the contacts bounced around at high speed, and to contain the problem the shafts had to be physically isolated from the rest of the Bombe apparatus. In sum, cobras were unreliable.

Another solution was put forward by the Post Office, whose team included Tommy Flowers, later to be the genius behind the Colossus machine at Bletchley Park (a project which has nothing to do with Enigma codebreaking even though its fame is comparable to that of the cryptanalytic attack on Enigma). Unfortunately, Flowers's first involvement in a Bletchley Park project was not a smooth experience; his team damaged a Bombe machine which they had borrowed for research purposes, a temporary loss which Bletchley could ill afford; and regrettable comments were made about the trusted BTM engineers, which were not calculated to endear the Post Office team to Bletchley Park's new management. Against this backdrop, it is a small miracle that the Post Office were allowed back in to work on Colossus.

The steadier approach of BTM and its chief engineer Doc Keen won out in the end. Keen understood that a much faster switching system was needed than the old-fashioned relays which provided the computing logic of the three-rotor Bombes. He was able to come up with an adaptation of the traditional Bombe which used super-fast relays for the testing needed on the fourth rotor – the 'High-Speed Keen'. Eventually, 56 of these fast Bombes would be put into production from February 1943.

The Bombe solution to the M4 Enigma took an inordinately long time, no doubt because of the disputatious nature of the process. For the whole of 1942 there was no four-rotor Bombe and a serious danger of no M4 decrypts.

A High-Speed Keen Bombe.

The U-boat *U-559* was on patrol off the coast of Egypt in the Mediterranean when she had the misfortune to be spotted by a Sunderland flying-boat on 30 October 1942. The Sunderland's crew radioed the position of the U-boat to the Royal Navy; destroyers happened to be nearby and rapidly reached the scene, locating the boat with their asdic (sonar) equipment. A depth-charge attack was inevitable, and its destructive effect forced the boat to the surface after ten hours of unimaginable torture for the boat's crew. Even on the surface the ordeal was not over: HMS *Petard* fired a shell at the boat's conning-tower. It was all up for the crew of *U-559*, who bundled over the side in the hope of rescue by one or other of their predators.

Meanwhile, a boarding-party had been mustered from volunteers on *Petard*, led by Lieutenant Tony Fasson. He boarded the sinking submarine together with Able Seaman Colin Grazier, while canteen assistant Tommy Brown, who was aged only 16, hung on outside to receive any booty handed up by the boarders. Fasson and Grazier knew what they were looking for – documents were the prize, and they needed to keep them dry even as the water levels rose in the doomed U-boat. Suddenly the boat took a lurch and plunged to the bottom. Brown got free in the *Petard*'s whaler with his precious haul, which in due time found its way to Bletchley Park. Fasson and Grazier lost their lives in the mission; they were posthumously awarded the George Cross. Brown received the George Medal, its youngest-ever recipient.

The precious papers included the *Geheimer Wetterundseeschlüssel der Kriegsmarine, Teil 2: Wetterkurzschlüssel* – the short weather signal codebook. The very thing that Bletchley Park needed to get back on top of Naval Enigma, a precious source of cribs that could be run on three-rotor Bombe machines while the civil war over the four-rotor Bombes played itself out. On 13 December 1942 Bletchley Park sent the Admiralty its estimate of the positions of 13 U-boats, the first location intelligence derived from Enigma for nine months. Bletchley Park was back in the game.

America joins the fight

The United States of America officially entered World War II with the attack on Pearl Harbor on 7 December 1941. Four days later, Germany declared war against the United States. But, if not exactly at war with Germany, America had been in an escalating conflict with Germany in the Atlantic for many months. Prime Minister Winston Churchill had badgered President Franklin D. Roosevelt for a 'destroyers for bases' deal back in 1940, so that Britain's famous Royal Navy, which was ludicrously weak when it came to convoy escort vessels, could try to improve its trade protection in return for the establishment of US bases in the Bahamas and the Caribbean. The Lend-Lease programme received Congressional sanction in March 1941. US merchant shipping was at risk from predation in the Atlantic as well as British, and US escort vessels joined the protective screens accompanying convoys from April 1941. Those vessels were not purely passive, and engaged in attacks on U-boats. It was evident to anyone who was watching that America was already committed on the Allied side.

In areas where no one should have been watching, America was also committed. The association began with an approach from the British, instigated by Winston Churchill in the summer of 1940, shortly after he became prime minister. The British scientist Sir Henry Tizard was sent over to America with the mission to entice the United States into a closer relationship. Britain was offering to show the Americans the technical progress it had made in a range of fields: radar, friend/foe aircraft recognition, the Whittle gas turbine and the top-secret 'Tube Alloys' project. Tube Alloys was the cover name for the British nuclear weapons programme, which must have seemed like complete and utter science fiction at that time. What was more realistic was the airborne IFF system, or 'identification of friend or foe' through radio signalling, an initiative which caught the imagination of General Joseph Mauborgne, the head of the US Army Signal Corps.

Once signals sent by the foe were in play it was a short step to communications intelligence, secrecy and detection and exploitation of the foe's own signals. The chief cryptanalyst of the US Army's Signals Intelligence Service, William F. Friedman, was roped in and tasked with developing a cryptanalytical exchange, much as the French and Poles had done with the British before the war broke out. Free transfer of technical know-how was, in a way, a free lunch; but no friend expects to be entertained indefinitely without returning hospitality in some form. Friedman's plan involved passing over to the British some of the priceless advances America had made against Japanese ciphers, in return for British information on its own greatest cryptanalytical secret – the secret of Enigma.

Out of these beginnings grew a plan to send a small team of American servicemen across the Atlantic to see for themselves what the British had achieved. By the end of 1940 the plan was more or less settled. The United States would be represented by two officers each from the army and the navy, and the gift of a Japanese cipher machine would be made to break the ice. The Japanese machine was, in fact, not Japanese at all: it was the creature of reverse-engineering by talented American codebreakers, who quite rightly for America's own security had been focusing on the threat from across the Pacific rather than what was going on in Europe. The machine itself reconstructed the function of the Japanese cipher machine codenamed 'Purple'; from the American perspective it was a gift of inestimable rarity and value.

The precious Purple machine was loaded on to HMS *King George V* for a rapid transit across the Atlantic in early 1941, accompanied by Abraham Sinkov and Leo Rosen (for the US Army) and Prescott Currier and Robert Weeks (for the US Navy). All four were relatively junior officers; Friedman had been laid up in hospital at the end of 1940 and his deputy could not be spared. Sinkov was a top-class codebreaker and Rosen was an expert with the Purple machine. The Naval team were less experienced, or at least in later years claimed to be so. Currier certainly had some expertise, but of the four any familiarity with the Enigma problem rested with Sinkov.

The voyage across the Atlantic was eventful for the American quartet. Not only were they on a full-scale British warship in commission, but they found themselves briefly under air attack at one stage. Nothing could be better calculated to underscore the peril in which Britain found herself in the first winter of the war in which she was fighting alone. The servicemen eventually reached Bletchley Park, after dark in the late afternoon of 8 February 1941. As with the rest of the country, everything was blacked out. Through the darkened hallway of the Bletchley Park mansion the four Americans were ushered into the office of Commander Alastair Denniston and plied with glasses of a somewhat unfamiliar aperitif, which turned out to be sherry. Of all ways to concoct a welcome this must rank as among the most bizarre; history does not relate whether it made the guests feel at home.

As their visit lengthened, it slowly dawned on the honoured visitors that they were being treated like royalty; once the sherry formalities were over they found themselves accommodated in grand style with the local gentry, wined and dined notwithstanding the privations of a country under siege. They were also shown all over the Bletchley site, over the interception and direction-finding facilities in various parts of the country, and given the complete picture of signals intelligence including organization, capture, decryption and creation of intelligence. They were let into the secrets of German, Italian and Russian codes and ciphers, and shown how punched-card apparatus could be used to speed up the sorting and analysis of enciphered material.

All the same, there was a problem. For one thing, the precious Purple machine seemed to have cut no ice with the British. While American histories focus on the significance of this handover, not just in terms of the earnestness of the gesture but also as a symbol of their own proficiency, it is almost invisible in the British record. The unspoken, unwritten expectation of the Americans was that if this was what they were willing to share, then the British for their part would surely reciprocate with their own greatest breakthrough. The invisibility of Purple implies that the significance was lost on the sherry-wielding British, who undoubtedly saw themselves as the senior partners in the relationship, and as seniors the ones who were in control. Japan was very far away, and a threat to Britain from that quarter in early 1941 was very remote. Controlling access to the

Enigma secret was the live issue, and the one of most important concern.

John Tiltman, by now a senior figure in the Bletchley establishment, was asked about this in an interview in 1978:

> The Enigma wasn't my job. It had an entirely separate staff and so on. But I tried to get [Denniston] to give way on this, but he wouldn't do it... So I got permission, and went up to see General Menzies [the head of MI6, Bletchley Park's parent organization] ... I said to him, 'Unless you give way over this and show the American Party, allow them to see all our work on the Enigma, I don't see how we are going to have any kind of successful collaboration...' General Menzies ... said, 'All right, but if you disclose it to them, they must sign a document which lists all the people to which they'll make the disclosure when they get back to Washington and any fresh spreading information must also be reported back to us, otherwise we won't do it.' They were junior officers, they didn't like having to make this sort of decision without being able to refer back. Eventually, after I'd left them alone for about an hour and a half, I went into see them and I said, 'You know, this is something you can't go away without, or the whole thing will break down.'

The British reluctance to disclose everything about Enigma was understandable. Britain was at war; America was not. American security was untried and untested, and Germans were still sniffing around in America gathering what they could find. It was a dilemma like that which had faced the Poles once international Enigma intelligence cooperation had been mooted two years previously. As with the later crisis of resourcing at Bletchley, though, once the issue came to the attention of Winston Churchill the decision was made.

The Americans were to be allowed to see everything. Prescott Currier recalled:

> We went everywhere, including Hut 6. We watched the operation of the bombe. We were told in great detail the solution of the Enigma, who worked on it, how the bombe worked, what they had to do in order to get a readable text. Bob Weeks and I were not Enigma mathematicians or cryptanalysts but Abe [Sinkov] and Leo Rosen were and it was left to them to do whatever would be done in making the necessary notes and records that we would take back with us.

Watching and noting was all very well, but the restrictive agreement signed by Weeks would store up trouble.

> For: Commander Denniston
> 3/3/41
> 1. We are in accord with the purport of your memorandum of today. We undertake to carry out all instructions for the preservation of the secrecy of the work mentioned, informing by word of mouth only the head of our section, Commander L.F. Safford, USN.
> 2. In connection with the naval aspects of the above work we deem it advisable to obtain the wiring of interest (i.e. the device on which Turing is working), and to disclose that only when it is decided to work on the problem. In such an event we shall observe all precautions and keep you informed of our actions...
>
> Respectfully,
R.H. Weeks

From the British viewpoint all that had been asked for, and more, had been given: the transfer of secrets was comprehensive and complete, and intelligence sharing with the Americans was a free-flowing two-way street. Yet this is not how it seemed.

It might be wrong to characterize Commander Laurance F. Safford, USN, credited by the NSA as being 'the father of US Navy cryptology', as an Anglophobe, but it seems that Safford had his suspicions about the British and their close-to-the-chest secrecy obsession. Worse, it seemed to Safford that the four-officer mission had contrived to return to America empty-handed. While the Americans had delivered an entire Purple machine, the British had delivered nothing: no Bombe, not even an Enigma machine. True, there were some documents and a 'paper Enigma', but these were no substitute for three-dimensional equipment. The suspicion that the British were still treating the Americans as inferior, as the junior partners condescendingly allowed just so many candies and no more, now took root.

The sour feeling was compounded when the 'paper Enigma' was investigated. What this curious phrase meant was that – given that Enigma machines were not exactly freely available in Britain, and those that existed were in full-time use at Bletchley Park – the British had given drawings and wiring diagrams to the Americans, so that the United States could manufacture its own machines. But the perfidious British had, it seemed, fouled up the drawings. It later transpired that a missing document had gone astray in Washington, but from here on the goal of cooperation on Enigma was beset with difficulty, misunderstanding, and fear of loss of control on both sides.

The difficulties were hardly helped by the American services' approach to organization, which was very hard for the British to comprehend. As was then common across many countries, naval codebreaking was handled separately from army codebreaking. To do justice to Safford, he was a prime contender for better cooperation between the two services; but for the duration of the war, American naval and army codebreaking would be separate concerns, even where common questions like the Enigma problem were involved.

The United States Navy had a first-class asset in the codebreaker Agnes Meyer Driscoll. Born in 1889, she joined the navy's Code and Signal Section for research work in 1918. Her job was to assess the US Navy's own codes and ciphers for security, teaching herself 'to be a codebreaker, to be a better code maker.' By World War II she was well established as the US Navy's foremost codebreaker, 'accomplishing the impossible' in breaking the Japanese navy's superenciphered operational 'Blue Book' code after its introduction in 1931, inventing her own cipher machines, and even solving a Japanese naval machine cipher using pencil-and-paper methods. After the return of Currier and Weeks, she turned her attention to Naval Enigma.

In August 1941, Alastair Denniston visited Washington in an effort to smooth the ruffled feathers and try to reset the cooperation arrangements. Mrs Driscoll told him how she was inventing new attacks based on eight-letter cribs which wouldn't need a Bombe to find the Enigma settings. Denniston was, like Driscoll, a codebreaker of the old school; although he was himself no master of the Enigma problem, he knew enough about the evolution of the attack on Enigma since the early days of pencil-and-paper attacks by Dilly Knox to be sceptical about her proposals. Partly this was because Mrs Driscoll's written questions about Enigma, which Denniston brought back with him, were very basic: there were things about the machine itself which still seemed to be a puzzle to her. Given the woeful state of British knowledge about the Enigma machine not much more than two years previously, it would be wrong to condemn Driscoll on this ground alone. The British answered her questions, feeling that it would be better if she visited Bletchley to get up to speed more directly; but the tone of the answers is that of an impatient parent. To take one example:

> The standard three-rotor Enigma machine has a curious stepping pattern, in that the middle rotor steps twice on successive key-strokes, owing to the fact that the pawl causing the stepping of the left-hand rotor also pushes the middle rotor when the stepping-notch on the middle rotor is in position to be acted upon. This behaviour is, perhaps, obvious to those who have studied the machine and its mechanism in detail. But it is sufficiently obscure to have merited a modern write-up in the learned journal *Cryptologia*. It is hardly a surprise that Mrs Driscoll hadn't grasped it, with only the 'paper Enigma' to work on, in the summer of 1941. Her fourth question was 'When the Middle Wheel makes an extra jump, is this a mechanical feature or is it done "Impromptu" by the encoding officer?'. The British response was not the three-page explanation set out in *Cryptologia*; they just said, 'Middle wheel extra jump is a mechanical feature.'

If this was typical of the way that reasonable American questions were going to be handled, it did not augur well for the 'special relationship'. The British, of course, did not appreciate that while the US Army had an actual commercial model Enigma machine, from which the stepping curiosity would have been evident, this machine was not available to the US Navy; Captain E.E. Hastings, the UK liaison officer in Washington had to warn Menzies, the head of MI6, that 'there is grave unrest' at the US Navy about how the British were behaving. The sense that the British were withholding something persisted almost until the end of the war; a supercilious response to Mrs Driscoll did not help. (On the other side, the US Navy wanted to build its own anti-Enigma capability, independent of British gifts and control; the pressure on Driscoll to deliver something was immense, and almost certainly impossible given the paucity of intercept material and general context available on the other side of the Atlantic.)

Still, Mrs Driscoll's cryptanalytical approach was based more in hope than reality. One method was to use a 'catalogue attack', not dissimilar to the **EINS** method used at Bletchley, where every single possible encipherment of a common word could be checked. Another used a squared-paper attack, not unlike Dilly Knox's original method which assumed no motion of the two slower rotors, and used a crib to find the setting. This was almost certainly doomed, since she had to assume additionally that the test letter in the crib was not cross-plugged to something else via the plugboard, which was only true for six out of 26 letters. The problem with each of these methods is that, without mechanization, the war would have been long over before any solution of a day's key could be produced.

The problem was not, as has been suggested, that Mrs Driscoll's faculties had been impaired by a shockingly awful car accident in 1937, in which she was seriously injured and two of her fellow passengers were killed. More likely it was that old-time codebreakers, just like Dilly Knox and W.F. Clarke at Bletchley Park, found the transition to the machine codebreaking era a big leap. Mrs Driscoll, unaided by the British, wasn't going to be able to make that jump. Perhaps, if she had been able to make the journey to Bletchley and talk to the statisticians there, things might have been different. When she met Alan Turing in Washington the following year, he said 'I was rather alarmed; she asked a great number of questions, to most of which fortunately I did not know the answers anyway, and told me very little, mostly I think because they weren't really doing anything.'

Shades, once again, of the British reluctance to engage fully and openly? That may be so, but Alan Turing's visit was focused on machine attacks on Enigma, and that wasn't the bailiwick of Agnes Meyer Driscoll. It seems likely that he only asked about the pencil-and-paper methods to see whether there actually had been any progress since Denniston's visit in 1941.

Although Driscoll was still stuck to her squared paper, things were very different over at the US Army. The mechanically-minded Rosen had absorbed everything he saw at Bletchley like a sponge, and what's more he saw ways to develop and exploit the Bombe approach in modern and exciting ways. The US Army put Rosen on to something called the 'Yellow' Project:

The cryptanalysis of the German Army and Air Force traffic was first considered by the [US Army's] Signal Intelligence Service in the early spring of 1942. The methods of Enigma cryptanalysis used by the Navy (OP-20-G) and at GCCS had been examined and it was decided to abandon the rotary type Bombe used at these centers in favor of a relay switching system which could be developed at the Bell Telephone Laboratories in New York.

Many years later, Rosen was asked why the US Army felt the need to build their own machine. Rosen explained:

Well, first of all, the British equipment needed improving, and secondly, we wanted an alternate piece of equipment away from the field in the event that there was a possible invasion of Great Britain. We would be completely out of business if we didn't have a backup system, and there was a need for an alternate site, so we felt compelled to build this system.

'Needed improving' was perhaps a little unfair. There wasn't much wrong with the British equipment, but Rosen was absolutely right that the American reworking of the Bombe could transform it to a much higher level of efficiency and versatility. The essential principle was the elimination of the rotating parts of the Bombe, and replacing them with a fully digital system created out of telephone relays. Bell Telephone Laboratories (Bell Labs) was the obvious place to do this, not simply because they had the telephone relay capability, but because their research facility in New York City was producing groundbreaking logical circuits, the basic components of computing systems. The brains behind the circuitry was the computer pioneer George W. Stibitz, who attended the first meeting with Rosen and Friedman on 30 September 1942.

Emulating Enigma rotors, which converted the 26 letters of the alphabet to a different letter, and then moved around to produce a different conversion, was just a matter of switching. The wiring inside each rotor, responsible for those conversions, could be achieved by three banks of three relays, which neatly gave 27 possible outputs. Once all the moving parts were replaced by digital logic systems, three benefits would flow. Firstly, the machine would be much faster than the rotary Bombe; secondly, manufacture and maintenance would be much easier, particularly as the machine was made from off-the-shelf components in factories needing no special security precautions; and thirdly, the digital-logical approach meant that the machine could accommodate changes like new rotors or additional rotors without requiring full-scale re-engineering. Better still, the machine could be enhanced with what, in a later era, would be called 'peripherals': not just printers (though the US Army Bombe had those), but codebreaking accessories for dealing automatically with false stops, or incomplete keys and such like problems. The only downside was that the relay-switching equipment took up a vast amount of space and electricity. The basic unit alone required 144 frames of electrical switching, and the finished machine occupied an entire hall.

The US Army machine was approaching readiness for operations by early 1943. By that time, relations between the Americans and the British had begun to thaw. Liaison meetings had been taking place during 1942. John Tiltman visited Washington at the end of March, though found himself tied in knots by the security precautions imposed by his superiors, which forbade him discussing Bletchley's problems with the new four-rotor Naval Enigma. Tiltman received a mauling from Admiral Joseph R. Redman, the new US Director of Naval Communications, about British failings on U-boat Enigma; it was clear that the US Navy planned to mount an attack of its own, with or without British help. Although Mrs Driscoll's attempt was hopeless (and Tiltman had to tell her so), the US Navy had shaken up the Communications Unit with the appointment of Redman, and one casualty had been the head of cryptographic research, Laurance F. Safford. With him replaced by Joseph N. Wenger, the way was open for new, more positive, approaches.

One new thing was a formal agreement between Wenger and Travis on division of labour between the two countries. The United States would target Japan, and the United Kingdom Germany, and each would leave the counterpart field clear for the other. Most of the time, that is; the Allies would cooperate on Enigma, and unwritten and unspoken clauses of the agreement were that, most of the time, each of the codebreaking agencies would look the other way if they found out that the others had trespassed into reserved territory. And the agreement was only about naval codebreaking, at least as far as the Americans were concerned, even if Travis had more comprehensive authority, and perhaps broader expectations.

Still, the new and somewhat unsatisfactory deal allowed for a new approach to the problem of Naval Enigma. The US Navy was going to design and build its own four-rotor Bombe, regardless of objections from the British. Secondly, there was a willingness to enter into constructive dialogue. Fortunately, Tiltman was able to persuade Sir Stewart Menzies of MI6 that the restrictions imposed on him, and the 'prohibition' disallowing the Americans to create their own Enigma-breaking facilities on US soil were unworkable. Moreover, at this time the management of Bletchley Park was itself being shaken up, and the more business-like Commander Edward Travis had taken over from Alastair Denniston. Travis and Wenger were able to do business; a series of agreements under which the roles and responsibilities of the two countries as regards codebreaking, and Enigma in particular, were thrashed out.

A material consequence of all this was that Americans began to arrive at Bletchley Park, first as observers, and by 1943 as fully-integrated contributors within the team. Sure, the Americans had their own command and reporting structures, but their involvement in the Enigma effort on both sides of the Atlantic was now assured.

As far as the US Navy's new attack on four-rotor M4 Enigma was concerned, the need for a machine solution was now fully accepted. The navy turned not to Bell Labs but to the National Cash Register Corporation in Dayton, Ohio, who counted among their staff the talented engineer Joseph R. Desch. Like Stibitz at Bell Labs, Desch had invented a form of calculator – but Desch's device was made from electronic components, not electromechanical relays. Desch's solution for the Bombe would address the need for speed through this new technology.

The Desch Bombe, when its design was finalized at the beginning of 1943, used Bletchley-style rotors to emulate the central part of the Enigma machine, though rotating at much higher speeds than the Bletchley machines could achieve. The problem this created was that of overshoot: when the Bombe detected a plausible set-up

Contrasting bombes. Above: US Navy Bombe;
below: US Army Bombe control room.

for the Enigma the rotors would continue to spin under their own momentum. Desch's answer was to incorporate a memory unit which would record the set-up electronically, so that the overshoot could be disregarded. The first of Joe Desch's machines became operational in May 1943 and were immediately successful in finding Enigma settings.

Creating the US Navy Bombe was, despite its ultimate success, not an easy project. As part of the renewed spirit of cooperation, Alan Turing was sent across to the United States in late 1942 to consult with Desch (as well as have his strange conversation with Agnes Meyer Driscoll). It seems that an early plan to have differently-sized rotors for the faster- and slower-spinning axles of the Bombe was abandoned as a result of Turing's advice. Turing spent a few days in Dayton, and from there he was due to go to New York to see the projects in development at Bell Labs.

One of those projects, of course, was the US Army Bombe. And here there was a new source of tension. For one thing, the British had still not discerned that the US Army was not the same thing as the US Navy, and that the naval clearance which Turing had received was worth nothing when it came to the army's projects. In second place, the development of a Bombe by the army was, at least to British eyes, a violation of the carefully agreed pact whereby the Americans could exploit British Enigma codebreaking ideas only in a limited way, for naval purposes. As far as German Army or air force Enigma was concerned, exploitation was something which should be going on at Bletchley Park or not at all. Thirdly, there was another project at Bell Labs – the development of a radio-telephone encryption device, which Alan Turing had specifically been tasked to inspect. That device was far beyond any agreements, and wholly off-limits, at least as far as the Americans were concerned.

But the British were not going to roll over. For the moment, and possibly for the last time, they were able to act as dominant partner in

Joseph R. Desch

Joseph Raymond Desch was born in Dayton, Ohio, about a mile from the bicycle shop owned by the Wright Brothers. In 1938, he joined the National Cash Register Corporation (NCR) which was based in the city. An early achievement was to build a digital electronic calculator – in 1940, when calculating machinery was still mechanical or relying on electrical relays, like the British Bombe. It was Desch's insight into the use of electronic valves or tubes for counting that led to his development of the American Bombe. Eventually 121 of his Bombes were produced. Unlike the British Bombe, American naval Bombes had 16 replica Enigmas (the British machines had 36), so were restricted to running one menu or rotor-order at a time; nevertheless, they could be coupled together to attack Enigma traffic which the British were unable to prioritize, notably the 'Seahorse' Enigma key used by German blockade-runners in the Far East.

In a curious twist, once the US Navy assigned NCR and Desch to the Bombe project, the facility was renamed the 'Naval Computing Machine Laboratory', anticipating the linkage between electronics, codebreaking and post-war computers. After the war, it was Desch who developed the first completely solid-state computer, and served as a member of the NSA's Scientific Advisory Board.

In 1947, Joe Desch received America's highest honour for civilian service, the National Medal of Merit. But because it was for secret work, he could not even tell his family why it had been awarded. Joe Desch died in 1987, by when the Enigma story had broken cover, and it was only then that his own distinctive contribution to the story began to be known. These days, there is a 'Joe Desch Award' for innovation in information technology, given by the Engineers Club of Dayton.

the US-UK relationship. An increasingly fraught exchange of letters between General George C. Marshall, the US Chief of Staff, and Field Marshal Sir John Dill, the British military liaison in Washington (and himself former Chief of the Imperial General Staff in London) got more and more tense. Dill finally snapped on 7 January 1943.

> It seems to me however that the proposals in your letter derogate from the principle of full reciprocity. Our position, I understand, had been made quite clear. We are prepared to show your people everything <u>in England</u>, but we reserve the right to refuse to allow 'exploitation' in the U.S. of vitally secret traffic where we are chiefly concerned, unless we are satisfied as to the necessity. We have, for example, permitted such 'exploitation' by the U.S. Navy in one particular type of traffic which we agreed was of vital importance to them.
>
> ... the refusal to permit Dr. Turing to have access ... is a new principle contrary to the spirit of existing agreements. It would seriously disturb our people at home and would of course involve the U.S. Navy who are very much dependent on free exchange with our people.

It was all about Enigma, and not at all about the phone encryption device. Either the Americans let Turing into Bell Labs, or they would be cut off completely from the source of signals intelligence which the British had completely mastered. The American response was swift. Alan Turing's clearance to visit Bell Labs was issued, and Enigma intelligence sharing would continue.

Friction continued alongside the sharing. Some of it stemmed from the US armed forces' continuing belief that the navy needed to defend itself against the army, and vice versa, with the United Kingdom being asked to get information through the back door which was refused through the front. There were requests for information (on both sides) which might not be justifiable and refusals as well. One important consideration for the British was to disabuse General George V. Strong, the head of the US Army's Signal Intelligence Service, that Bletchley Park was the only location from which the British war against Enigma could be waged.

In fact, the British had readily foreseen the need for distributing the Bombes across several sites, in case of aerial attack. By mid-1943 there were Bombes at Adstock Manor, Wavendon and Gayhurst Manor – all in the vicinity of Bletchley – and two new large facilities were in development. The first, at Stanmore on the fringes of North London, was by far the largest in 1943, and would grow to house over 70 Bombes by the war's end. But even Stanmore was overtaken by Eastcote, also near London. Eastcote was just beginning operations in 1943; by 1945 it housed over 100 Bombes, and in due course became the headquarters of GCHQ, when the Government Code & Cypher School changed its name and moved out of Bletchley Park.

Although the multiplicity of sites might have been a good argument that a backup centre in the United States for attacking German Army and Air Force Enigma was needless, especially since the threat of a German invasion of Britain now seemed a very remote possibility, the legalistic arguments were irrelevant to the main point. That point was that the British were still trying to hang on to their monopoly over Enigma codebreaking, and were reluctant to accept the reality that it was a thing of the past. The Americans had far more economic and military muscle than the beleaguered British, and the monopoly had been ceded back in 1941 when Rosen and Sinkov had been shown the secrets of Bombe technology.

Still, the British were going to have one last try. General Strong himself visited Bletchley Park in the summer of 1943. Strong – in stark contradistinction to his erstwhile opposite number Safford in the US Navy – was a vigorous supporter of Anglo-American cooperation. His visit was a peace mission, an effort to make the alliance work in practice despite all the bickering, misunderstanding and game-playing. Strong's visit included, naturally enough, a discussion or two with Commander Travis's 'Assistant Director' – a title which perhaps failed to convey that its bearer was Travis's Executive Officer, in charge of all things. This was none other than the formidable and clever Nigel de Grey, a veteran of World War I codebreaking (whose CV included, alongside Dilly Knox, the successful attack on the 'Zimmermann Telegram' whose breaking was instrumental in the United States becoming engaged in that war). De Grey concealed his cold steel behind a façade which owed more to his inter-war career as art historian and curator than bureaucrat; at the end of the meeting, Strong had been charmed into making another cooperation agreement with the British. The gist of it that raw Enigma decrypts should on no account be sent by the Americans working at Bletchley direct to Washington; they could be worked on and analysed and paraphrased and digested, but only in the UK, and the General Staff and Military Intelligence and War Department and anyone else in Washington who might be interested in the content of these messages could make do with processed food.

On his return home, Strong was in no doubt that he'd been bamboozled. Sure, the British had a point, which was that the security of the source might be imperilled by the free retransmission of verbatim Enigma texts, especially over American systems which were known to be read by the Germans themselves. But there were answers to the security problem and no excuses for keeping the American decision-makers out of the loop. It was the last gasp of British supremacy over Enigma, and it couldn't last.

Over in Washington, both the US Army and the US Navy had been scaling up their capability. New sites were acquired. In June 1942 the army took over the Arlington Hall Junior College for Women, situated just over the river from the city itself, to house the Signals Intelligence Service. Later in the year the navy moved into the Mount Vernon Seminary for Girls, situated on Nebraska Avenue in North West Washington, DC. These large academy buildings were suitable for very large administrative facilities which were destined to accommodate thousands of office workers.

The numbers tell the story. Whereas the doughty Gustave Bertrand had had six people on his tiny staff back in 1939, when the Polish, French and British codebreakers first met to discuss the problem of Enigma, and the Polish team counted 14 codebreakers when they reassembled in France secretly in 1942, the Government Code & Cypher School had 9,000 staff by 1943. That might seem a large number; it was certainly exponential growth from the few hundred who had formed the nucleus of the British codebreaking function at the beginning of the war. But even the GC&CS number paled into the shadows when the number of personnel deployed by the United States in their two former girls' schools are measured. At the peak in 1945, the number of people involved was around 14,000. Needless to say, not all of these people – in any of these organizations – were working on Enigma. But many were, and America's contribution to the Enigma story cannot be belittled.

One hundred and twenty-one US Naval Bombes were brought into operation before the war's end. Those machines did not just help with convoy routeing and U-boat evasion. The American approach was to take the war to the enemy. Beginning in 1943, the aggressive use of Enigma intelligence allowed the US Navy to target the all-important refuelling ships on which the U-boats depended for their extended Atlantic patrols. Called 'milch cows', in a Biblical reference, the ships in question were themselves a specially designed version of the U-boat which could carry fuel and other supplies under water

Workers at SIS in Arlington Hall, 1944.

to their thirsty clients. But with the aid of Joe Desch's Bombes, the refuelling rendezvous locations were disclosed to the codebreakers, who informed the operations branch, who in turn sent out destroyers to intercept and sink every craft, both attack U-boat and milch cow, they could find. By the last year of the war, the old-fashioned U-boat was a spent force.

The one risk – rarely admitted in history books – of such huge expenditure of money and personnel against the Enigma challenge was that the Germans might change their encipherment system. Aggressive use of Enigma intelligence in the manner of the milch cow attacks might give the game away, and force a change which, now, no one on the Allied side wanted to see. The question, in fact, was not whether the Germans would change the system, but when and how.

U-571 and U-505

Captures of U-boats – with the possibility of recovering 'confidential books', the secret documents containing Enigma settings, bigram tables, short weather codes and other material of value to the Allied codebreakers – happened on several occasions in World War II. *U-110* was boarded and cipher material retrieved before she sank on 9 May 1942. *U-559* was the U-boat boarded in October of that year, with the capture of the weather codebook which enabled Bletchley Park to restart the fight against Naval Enigma. Perhaps the oddest U-boat capture was that of *U-570*, which surrendered to an aircraft on 27 August 1941, although by the time a Royal Navy ship could come alongside to take possession of the prize the confidential books had long been destroyed.

A more celebrated case is that of *U-571*. If you believe what you see in the movies, the capture of *U-571* by the US Navy resulted in the retrieval of an Enigma machine and thereby provided the United States with an example of this hitherto unknown device, and thereby enabled the breaking of Enigma messages to take place. Unfortunately, the truth is a bit more prosaic. *U-571* was sunk by an Australian Sunderland aircraft off the west of Ireland on 28 January 1944 with the loss of all hands. Nothing was captured. And by then the Americans had plenty of Enigma machines and the knowledge of how to break Enigma messages.

The Hollywood film of *U-571* seems to be based on an actual episode which was every bit as dramatic as the film script, without the need for embellishment. Captain Daniel V. Gallery USN was determined to capture a U-boat, and as commanding officer of a hunter-killer task group whose role was to seek out and destroy U-boats he was well placed to give this a try. On 4 June 1944 his force came upon *U-505* off the west coast of Africa, and was able to force her surrender without the boat being scuttled or the confidential books and materials being jettisoned or destroyed. Gallery had the *U-505* towed all the way to Bermuda under conditions of strictest secrecy.

Among the 500kg (1,100 pounds) of documents retrieved from the U-boat were many gems of crucial intelligence value: not only were there cipher documents, but information on (and examples of) the new acoustic homing torpedo recently introduced to the German armoury, details of the 'snorkel' system which enabled U-boats to stay submerged for longer periods, and other technical details. The cipher materials were the U-boat Enigma keys for June 1944 for the Atlantic and Indian Oceans, a grid chart cipher – the Germans encoded location information, not only by using a 'grid square' numbering system instead of latitude and longitude, but then by disguising the grid square numbers – a short signal cipher, bigram tables, and the short weather signals cipher. And there were two Enigma machines. While it would be hard to claim that the capture of *U-505*'s cipher materials constituted a turning-point in the fight against Enigma, they were undoubtedly helpful, in particular by saving time. The short signal cipher was an extra layer of security above that provided by Enigma. To decrypt these messages both the daily Enigma key and the cipher needed to be recovered – when a new book was introduced, up to half a day's extra delay would arise before German signals in this cipher could be read, a delay which would now not occur.

Furthermore, according to a US Navy appreciation:

The Atlantic and Indian Ocean U-boat cipher keys were delivered to Op-20-G [the US Navy's codebreaking department] on 12 June. As a result, from 13 to 30 June we were able to read all messages in this cipher as soon as the Germans were ...

4,000 extra bombe hours were run by Op-20-G on Mediterranean keys which would normally have been run on British bombes. This permitted GC&CS to spend an equivalent amount of time on Army and Air Force keys...

Clearly, by June 1944 the US Navy's cryptological standoff against the US Army seems to have been resolved.

The story of *U-505* has a splendid sequel. She is now on display at the Chicago Museum of Science and Industry, preserved intact and able to be visited by the public. Only four U-boats survive from the war, and perhaps the most important legacy of Gallery's ambition to capture a U-boat is this.

CHAPTER EIGHT

The last Enigmas

Enigma was not an invention that stood still. As we have already seen, modified versions of the Enigma machine were brought into service for the Abwehr and for the German Navy; these were not the only different forms of Enigma. At the museum at Bletchley Park half-a-dozen or more examples of Enigma machines from different branches of the family, created for all sorts of purposes, are on display. But as far as the German armed forces were concerned, the basic model of Enigma machine with its three (or, in the German Navy from 1942, four) rotors remained in use for the duration of the war. This posed a serious security risk: the capture of a machine and its rotors was a virtual certainty, and for the German Army and air force the only defence against Bletchley Park and Arlington Hall was the procedure for setting the key.

Unsurprisingly, against this background the Germans concluded that structural modifications to their most heavily-used cipher machine were desirable. A number of changes were proposed, and some were brought into operation before the year's end. The first of these was Uncle Dick.

The turnaround wheel, known in the German language as the *Umkehrwalze*, was nicknamed 'Uncle Walter' by the British. Some time in 1943 intelligence reached Bletchley Park that a new type of turnaround wheel, the *Umkehrwalze-D* or UKW-D, was going to be introduced on some networks. This device became known as Uncle Dick. The nickname fitted well: to the Germans, it was 'Dora', and people of the Bletchley Park generation had been brought up on primary-school reading books featuring children called Dick and Dora. So, it had to be Uncle Dick.

But Uncle Dick was not an avuncular figure. The cipher machine expert Philip Marks says that 'UKW-D represented a significant improvement to the cryptographic security of the Enigma, and it presented a major threat to Bletchley's grip on the Enigma traffic of the [German Air Force].' Given that the 'Red' air force key was the lynchpin of Enigma codebreaking at Bletchley – a powerful source of cribs for other networks as well as a useful source in its own right – the introduction of this accessory posed a substantial challenge to the intelligence machine that Bletchley had become.

Uncle Dick was a turnaround wheel which could be removed from the Enigma machine so that its internal electrical links could be changed. It was, in effect, like having a second plugboard but within the heart of the rotary-scrambler unit of the Enigma machine. At a stroke Uncle Dick could render all the rotary Bombe machines in use obsolete. The first intimations of the new wheel came in a message dated 27 December 1943. For reasons unknown, the German operator sent the message in clear language, and it asked whether the receiver had been supplied with *Umkehrwalze Dora*. Something nasty was obviously afoot. On 1 January 1944 it first came into operation, on the all-important Red key, but only in Scandinavia and France. Rollout elsewhere and on other networks was slow, however, and fortunately for the codebreakers the operating instructions only required the wheel wiring to be changed every ten days or so. This was probably because the adjustment was fiddly and difficult, with the risk of errors, but still the new arrangement posed a major problem for Bletchley.

Certainly techniques were known for recovering the wiring structure of turnaround wheels, but with this changing so frequently against a backdrop of daily alteration of the basic settings like plugboard connections and rotor choice, the challenge should not be underestimated. It would not be until the late autumn of 1944 that the codebreakers got on top of the problem. In true British style a committee was established to tackle it; and ultimately a machine solution presented itself.

The simplest way to confront Uncle Dick was when some networks were using the old turnaround wheel, UKW-B. The settings for messages enciphered by networks using UKW-B could be determined by traditional Bombe methods; sometimes the same settings (plugboard, rotor choice and ring-settings) were also being used on networks which had converted to UKW-D. That gave a way in, using a crib, to finding the cross-wiring pattern in UKW-D.

Fortunately, as it turned out, the cryptanalysis of Uncle Dick was less troublesome than it should have been. Uncle Dick was reserved for special cases, and that meant that sometimes the same settings were used for the important Uncle Dick messages as well as the lesser ones; the only difference was the UKW-D pairings, and as Philip Marks says, 'this was a catastrophic error, as it enabled Hut 6 to break a daily key in the normal way using cribs and Bombes.'

Uncle Dick – the UKW-D turnaround wheel with alterable cross-wiring.

In addition, the US Army and US Navy were able to adapt their mechanized approaches to Enigma codebreaking to meet the challenge of UKW-D head on. The versatile US Army Bombe could add in peripheral units to carry out additional logic tests: essentially dealing with UKW-D was a problem in programming, and once the program was designed the extra racks of relays and wiring could be brought into the Bombe facility to carry out the additional task. In the case of UKW-D, the add-on units were called 'autoscritchers', and came into operation in early 1945. The British Uncle Dick Committee gave the American device the cover name 'Pepsi-Cola'; when it was replaced, some time later, by a faster machine officially called the 'superscritcher', that became 'Coca-Cola'.

For their part, the US Navy had been unable to ignore UKW-D, since indications had also been given in 1943 that U-boats were going to be equipped with it. As things turned out, UKW-D was only used in naval contexts when it was necessary to communicate with the German Air Force, but in the meantime the threat could not be disregarded. But it was not a quantum leap in difficulty for the navy, as the settable fourth rotor and interchangeable reflectors brought into use for the M4 version of Enigma was analytically very similar, and that was a problem which was well in hand. The navy's answer to UKW-D specifically was an automated device whose principle was similar to that for checking plugboard pairings. If a crib, coupled with a Bombe-generated plugboard prediction, indicated that the letter **G** was plugged to **R**, the same crib and Enigma settings could not logically allow that **R** be plugged to **Y**. Inconsistencies like this allowed for what the codebreakers called 'Stecker knock-out', from the German word for plug. Stecker knock-out – inconsistency, based on the crib, of putative pluggings – could be used to test a prediction about the plugging used in UKW-D in the same way. The US Navy, like their army counterparts, opted for a machine solution, and once again they chose to make use of electronic components to help speed up the machine. They called it 'Duenna', and the prototype came into operation late in 1944.

Duenna illustrates how transatlantic cooperation had matured since the difficult days of 1942. The design of Duenna was heavily influenced by the British codebreaker Hugh Alexander, who had taken over the running of Bletchley's Hut 8 from Alan Turing. Material and menus for Duenna were provided by the British; and likewise, across town at Arlington Hall, the work plan for the army's autoscritcher was agreed in cooperation with the British. By the time Uncle Dick was in wide use, the German Air Force was largely defeated, and the end of the war in Europe was in sight.

The German Air Force had evidently found Uncle Dick difficult to deploy, and had much the same trouble with another Enigma innovation which was called the *Uhr*, meaning clock. Stuart Milner-Barry, leader of Hut 6 at Bletchley, reported to the head of MI6 on this new modification:

This new gadget – apart from the short-lived Uncle Charlie [turnaround wheel C] and Uncle Dick, the only alteration in the actual Enigma machine introduced by the enemy during the whole course of the war – was sprung on us with no warning whatever... The first we knew of this new horror was the actual receipt of a number of messages on July 10 [1944], which began with a number and then went off into nonsense; together with a decode which referred to certain messages being encoded with 'Enigma Uhr', whatever that might be.

The *Uhr* was a small device which had its own wooden box, and which connected externally to a regular Enigma machine. It was called the clock because its central component was a circular dial like a clockface. The dial was the front face of a scrambler which had 40 electrical contacts arranged in a circle, with another 40 in a smaller circle just inside it. The contacts were cross-connected, so that electric current entering at outer contact 0 would emerge at inner contact 6, current entering at outer contact 1 emerged at inner contact 31, and so forth. The inner and outer contacts were connected to the Enigma machine using 20 cables which fitted into the plugboard – so the *Uhr* replaced the function of the plugboard with a variable cross-wiring which depended on which plugboard letter was connected to which contact on the clockface of the *Uhr*. Above the clockface was a wooden knob by which the operator rotated the clockface between messages so that a different scrambling pattern was in use every time a new message was sent.

The two-digit number which Milner-Barry had mentioned as appearing at the beginning of the offending messages was the information to the recipient of the message, telling him what *Uhr* setting to use.

Enigma Uhr.

From the cryptographic point of view, the *Uhr* did away with the single valid-for-a-day cross-wiring of the plugboard, making a new cross-wiring pattern possible for every message. Worse, it did away with the diagonal board, the modification of the British Bombe introduced by Gordon Welchman which had made the Bombes so efficient. The diagonal board worked because Welchman had discerned that if **A** was cross-plugged to **Q**, then **Q** was cross-plugged to **A**; the wiring in the *Uhr* was not reciprocal in this way, so that an input from **A** could indeed generate an output at **Q**, but without necessarily meaning that an input at **Q** generated an output at **A**: everything depended on the wiring between the inner and outer contacts on the *Uhr*'s scrambler.

On the other hand, there was only one pattern of wiring in the new *Uhr* scrambler, so there were fewer *Uhr* permutations, and once the wiring of the *Uhr* had been recovered the system was easy to break. And although the diagonal board was a component of vast importance in Bombe design, it was not fatal to have to remove it. As in the earliest days of Enigma-breaking with the first Bombe at Bletchley Park, what was needed was a clever choice of menus with plenty of loops in order to get a manageable number of 'stops', that is to say plausible rotor combinations. All this meant that Milner-Barry's report, dated only ten days after the 'horror' had manifested itself, expressed confidence that *Uhr* would not really pose a problem for Bletchley Park.

Surprisingly, perhaps, in this context, the German Air Force preferred the *Uhr* to UKW-D. There are suggestions that they thought it was cryptographically at least as good, and possibly better, which wasn't the case. But undoubtedly the *Uhr* was easier to use, and no code or cipher which is hard to use in the field will ever be secure since operators will take short-cuts, including even the use of plain language, if an emergency means that the system is too troublesome. By the summer of 1944, on the Eastern Front where the *Uhr* was principally deployed, it was an emergency all the time.

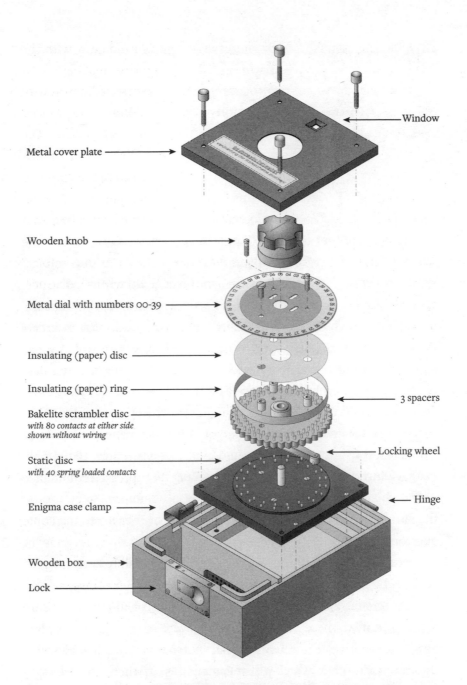

Window

Metal cover plate

Wooden knob

Metal dial with numbers 00-39

Insulating (paper) disc

Insulating (paper) ring

3 spacers

Bakelite scrambler disc
with 80 contacts at either side
shown without wiring

Locking wheel

Static disc
with 40 spring loaded contacts

Enigma case clamp

Hinge

Wooden box

Lock

Diagram showing the internal structure of the Enigma Uhr.

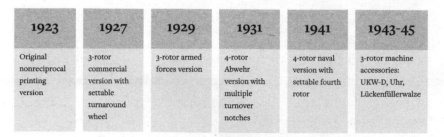

1923	1927	1929	1931	1941	1943-45
Original nonreciprocal printing version	3-rotor commercial version with settable turnaround wheel	3-rotor armed forces version	4-rotor Abwehr version with multiple turnover notches	4-rotor naval version with settable fourth rotor	3-rotor machine accessories: UKW-D, Uhr, Lückenfüllerwalze

Development of major Enigma variants.

The unending state of emergency towards the end of the war thwarted the rollout of one further change to the Enigma machinery which might, in the final analysis, have spelt doom to the factory-style processing of Enigma messages in the huge Bombe installations around London and Washington. This was the *Lückenfüllerwalze*, or variable-notch rotor. The design of good menus for Bombes depended on a tolerable stretch of letters in the crib which were sufficiently close together to make it unlikely that the middle rotor of the Enigma machine had stepped on to its next position during the sequence. A crib using a sequence of 13 or more letters posed the risk that a turnover of the middle rotor would happen somewhere, which would result in any 'stops' generated by the Bombe being useless. All of that hinged on the simple fact that Enigma rotors generally had only a single turnover notch, so that the permutation structure of the fast right-hand rotor was the only variable over each stretch of 26 enciphered letters.

Certainly, the German Navy's three additional rotors – never adopted by the air force or army – had extra turnover notches, and the Abwehr version of the Enigma had literally dozens of notches in its four rotors. But in all these cases the notches were in fixed positions; the navy rotors with two notches had their notches located diametrically opposite each other, which just meant that stepping happened after 13 letters rather than 26, so it wasn't a particularly sophisticated modification. The clever idea of the variable-notch rotor was that the notch positioning could be changed by the operator – adding or taking out notches, and thereby randomizing the stepping pattern of the rotors in the machine. The stepping pattern was altered simply by pushing a pin on the face of the rotor, to create an extra notch. Irregularity was achieved by picking a number of notches which was different for each rotor, a prime number, and not too many – or the issues with the Abwehr Enigma, which was broken by hand methods exploiting the simultaneous turnover of several rotors would recur.

The variable-notch rotor was developed and ready for production by early 1943. But it took until the near-miss assassination attempt against Hitler in July 1944, which was followed by a shakeup of the German signals organization, for the possibility of a rollout to be taken seriously. By the time adoption and production were approved in early 1945, it was far too late, and the new rotor never made it to the front line.

What this story of adaptations of Enigma leads to is the question why the German military authorities allowed a piece of technology originally developed for them in the mid-1920s to remain in use, with so little change, for almost 20 years. Surely, one assumes, there must

Enigma machine production
23,000 machines for the Germany Army and Air Force
12,000 machines for the German Navy
13,000 commercial model machines
350 Abwehr machines
318 Enigma machines of all types still in existence
Estimating the number of machines produced is extremely difficult. Records captured at the German factories where Enigma machines were manufactured help, and the serial numbers of machines are also useful. The figures given here are derived from data presented at www.cryptocellar.org and www.drenigma.org.

have been doubts about Enigma? Surely there must have been other systems which could have been used? And did the Germans never suspect that their principal system for enciphering secret signals had been compromised?

It is rarely appreciated on the Allied side that the answer to each of these questions is Yes. Perhaps the best known of the German doubts about Enigma is that in the U-boat arm, Admiral Dönitz had concerns from May 1940, and possibly earlier: the losses of U-boats in shallow waters suggested the risk of compromise. His concerns were not overlooked, but the signals security experts recognized that the issue was not the capture of an Enigma machine – something that would happen sooner or later – but the security of the 'key', or the daily set-up data.

To protect the key there was more than the complex bigram-table code for message settings and the printing of settings-sheets in water-soluble ink: there was the card-trick. If U-boat headquarters thought that a U-boat had been captured and its key-sheets might have been seized, the key could be switched instantly by the broadcast of a single trick-word or *Stichwort*. The captain of each U-boat had to memorize exactly what to do when a trick-word was received, and in some cases that what-to-do was extremely involved. Each part of the daily key – the rotor choices, the plugboard settings, the ring-settings – might have to be changed in some way through an arithmetical process or by transposing some of the data in the key-sheet.

Notwithstanding this security procedure, Dönitz continued to have concerns. Sometimes it seemed just too much of a coincidence that the British knew how to locate his U-boats. Radio transmissions from U-boats seemed to be to blame, and there was a debate on whether it was possible for the British to have refined radio direction-finding techniques to pinpoint U-boats (they had; direction-finding equipment was installed on ships, massively improving the accuracy of locating enemy craft). U-boat reports were reformed so that signals were reduced in length, so as to avoid long bouts of transmission which would facilitate direction-finding. The short signals could, when decoded, still contain substantial amounts of information. Even so, Dönitz remained concerned about the content as well as the utterance of radio signals. A U-boat rendezvous at sea in September 1941 was intercepted by the British, and there were other too-good-to-be-true 'coincidences'. Investigations which looked at Enigma security as well as other possible causes took place in 1941, 1942, 1943 and 1944. In every case there were good reasons to exonerate the cipher system.

What underlay the German conclusions from these probes was, in part, the fact that the Germans could see, in clear focus and minute detail, the British plans for convoy routeing. All the information they could possibly have needed was transmitted by radio in code disguised by weak ciphers which the Germans had mastered well before the outbreak of war. The few changes that had been implemented on the British side were not thorough enough to knock out the German codebreakers. Who would conclude that an enemy whose cipher security was so feeble could at the same time conquer the best machine cipher system ever devised?

By 1943, though, things had begun to change. It was slowly dawning on the British – mainly as a result of deciphering Enigma messages – that the Germans knew what the British were saying to each other, and thus that the Allied convoy ciphers were compromised. Change was on the way. At around this time the four-rotor Bombes began to deliver their goods, and improved weaponry, improved tactics, better radar and direction-finding, and above all more comprehensive air-cover made U-boat attacks on convoys much harder than before. The Allies switched to a new cipher system which the German codebreakers could not overcome. By May 1943, Dönitz concluded that the Atlantic U-boat war was a failure, and while U-boats never ceased to pose a threat, from this point on the war of codes at sea was definitively lost. While the question of Enigma's security never went away, it had ceased to be the issue of importance it had been in the first years of the war.

Less well known than the naval struggle with signals security is the parallel debate going on within the other codebreaking agencies of World War II Germany. Germany had many of these agencies, and enquiries into the robustness of Enigma were conducted by the Foreign Office and the Armed Forces Supreme Command; but the codebreakers of the German Army's High Command were constantly vigilant about Enigma, frequently proposing improvements and upgrades. It is their team that scrapped the double encipherment of the message setting in 1940, rendering the Polish anti-Enigma techniques obsolete overnight. They also developed new devices for sending enciphered messages and kept the danger of Enigma insecurity on the agenda for most of the war. A dedicated team of Germany's own codebreakers was assigned to study its vulnerability, and its work culminated in the production and rollout of the Enigma accessories described at the beginning of this chapter.

All that makes the question – as with the German Navy – why the German Army and air force stuck so obstinately to the Enigma system even more difficult. To begin with, it seems that the reports on Enigma's security were highly technical, filled with mathematical analysis and equations – not the kind of thing which is going to appeal to the military mind. It seems that the officer in charge of the army codebreaking section dutifully reported to his superiors that the investigations were going on, and when they had concluded, but the digests of the technical reports did not come across as a warning that the system was insecure.

Meanwhile – in contrast to the war at sea – on land the German military machine was unstoppable. After the overrunning of Poland, a swathe of northwestern European countries collapsed. Soon it was the turn of the Soviet Union, with areas the size of whole countries falling in a matter of weeks. Even in North Africa the apparently invincible Rommel pushed the British back almost to the Nile. Who needed to fuss and fret about cipher security while all this was going on? And from the other side, the German codebreakers themselves were able to glean plenty of information from low-grade codes and ciphers used by their enemies: one after another, the Germans had obtained intelligence of tactical value from Polish, French, British, Russian and, in time, American units. They proved that the value of codebreaking came from frontline battlefield units which were able to listen in, decode and pass to operational units the information of local and immediate value: it was speedy and efficient to do things in this decentralized way.

As to broader information of more strategic value, the British Army and Royal Air Force relied on more secure systems which the Germans found harder to break. The principal high-grade British system was called Typex. Typex was itself an Enigma derivative, using the same system of scrambler rotors connected electrically to a keyboard via a patch panel which was functionally equivalent to the plugboard on an Enigma. The name came from a 'Type X attachment', for printing out the cipher-text on paper strips. Typex also had an additional patch panel doing, more or less, the job which later came to be carried out for Enigma by Uncle Dick. The German codebreakers found Typex daunting because it had many more rotors than Enigma, and there were so few Typex machines in use in combat zones that they seem not to have been able to capture a complete set-up. In some minds the impossibility of the Typex challenge reinforced the mindset of Enigma's invulnerability.

Not everyone in German codebreaking circles thought that way. New recruits to the army's High Command codebreakers wanted to study Enigma afresh; advances in codebreaking techniques, particularly the use of punched card technology to speed up searching, suggested that relying on a very large number of permutations might be insufficient to protect the key. Moreover, parallel studies on other German cipher machine equipment indicated that these other systems, notably the T-52 combined teleprinter-and-cipher machine, were insecure. And to cap it all, a slow-moving investigation into the apparent success of the Polish codebreakers against Enigma before the war showed conclusively that the Enigma had, at one time, been cracked. The head of German Army Signals, General Fellgiebel, called a conference in April 1943, and decisions were taken. Improvements to Enigma and other cipher machines were to be put in hand. Instead of the unsafe T-52 the Enigma was to be used. For, the conference concluded, 'The cipher machine with plugboard is secure, so long as the enemy cannot get his hands on 20,000 letters enciphered at the same setting'. In October, the cipher security group summarized the situation on cipher machines:

Enigma. Various types: Plugboard Enigma, Counter Enigma [the Abwehr version], K=machine [the commercial model].

Plugboard Enigma in military units

Counter Enigma in Abwehr radio
} secure with correct use

K=machine or commercial machine   not secure.

It is not clear exactly what improvements General Fellgiebel ordained in 1943, but presumably the rollout of Uncle Dick and the *Uhr* were among them. By the time the Armed Forces cipher services were reshuffled in the summer of 1944, Fellgiebel was gone, and the whole thing was re-examined afresh, with yet another report on the security of Enigma. When this was all assessed at the turn of the year 1944-

45, it was far too late to do anything about it; Germany's last-ditch offensive in the west had failed, and the Red Army was advancing remorselessly from the east.

Once the war was over, the Allies – or rather, insofar as records are accessible, the British and American occupying forces – mounted their own investigation into Germany's cryptographic and cryptanalytical capabilities. The programme was codenamed TICOM, standing, with suitable obscurity as to its real purpose, for 'Target Intelligence Committee'. This multi-year project of interviewing prisoners and detainees, examining installations, scrutinizing and translating captured documents and making reports, covered everything from Germany's own codebreaking abilities to the problems of Enigma and its security – and of course the vital question whether the Germans knew that Enigma had been read, one way or another, for the whole duration of the war. What they learned must have been greatly reassuring. None of the papers gave the slightest hint that the Germans knew Enigma was fatally compromised. Sure, the various German investigations revealed weaknesses; but nothing conclusively showed that the Allies had had anything but one-off or fortuitous successes. Indeed, as one of the detainees lamented, the German codebreakers testing cipher security

> always wanted to work on their own traffic just as they would on foreign material, but were never given the opportunity. They never knew how the Army actually used the systems which they put out and they never saw any real traffic. When they asked for real traffic, they were given specifically prepared messages, one of which read: 'We are standing in Berlin and see the Polish infantry coming down the Frankfurter Allee'.

While the TICOM teams did not specifically have the brief to seize Enigma machines, it seems inevitable that many of them were seized when the German armies surrendered in 1945. The fate of the Enigma machines has been the subject of much speculation, though few concrete facts are discernible from archive materials. Certainly a goodly number, including some curious variants on the basic Enigma models, found their way to GCHQ, which emerged after the end of the war as the successor to Bletchley Park. One interesting suggestion is that the Allied governments sold Enigma machines to the governments of developing nations, suggesting that they were secure, while knowing all along that the sellers had means of breaking the cipher. More certain is the story that some countries in Europe continued to use Enigmas as the basis of their secure communications: in particular, the East German police continued to use Enigma after the onset of the Cold War, and the Western powers continued to break their messages.

Another suggestion connected with the post-war history of Enigma is that the Bombe machines were broken up. This is more dubious. What is known is that some of the Wrens who were, during the years of conflict, operators of these machines, were redeployed to dismantle Bombes so that their parts could be salvaged. That, however, does not exclude the possibility that some Bombes were kept in service, for example for the purposes of deciphering East German police messages. According to a document declassified only in 2007, 'the content of the communications carried on [the East German police system] could be described as mundane at best. It contained fire damage reports, state of readiness of various fire stations and police reports, mostly regarding insignificant arrests.' This was not the stuff by which the Cold War was going to be won.

Then one day in 1956 Ellie Carmen Klitzke, chief of the East German cryptanalytic section located in A Building at Arlington Hall Station, notified Preston Welch that the effort on Enigma was to be terminated. Preston was the cryptanalyst in charge of developing 'menus' to be run on the bombe... With a modest degree of fanfare, Preston held up a package and announced that it contained the last menus to be run on the bombe. He handed the package to a cryptanalytic intern who caught the shuttle bus from Arlington Hall Station to the Naval Security Station and delivered the menus to the Navy Waves who ran the bombe. They in turn ran the machine for the last time.

The last of the World War II Bombes is a four-rotor Desch-type machine, now a museum exhibit at the National Cryptologic Museum, in Fort Meade, Maryland. No others survive, but a remarkable project initiated by retired engineer John Harper in Britain in 1995 led to the reconstruction of a fully working three-rotor Turing-Welchman Bombe which is regularly demonstrated and explained to visitors at The National Museum of Computing located at Bletchley Park.

For Sale	Enigma machines past and present	
Date	Details	Price in USD
1941	New Enigma machine, 3-rotor plugboard model, factory price RM 800	2,000
2012	3-rotor machine sold at auction	84,000
2017	3-rotor machine bought in fleamarket in Romania for $114 then re-sold	51,620
2018	4-rotor machine in perfect condition, together with accessories, sold at auction: the 17th most costly scientific artefact sold at auction that year	444,500
2020	Completely corroded 3-rotor machine beyond repair sold at auction	45,500

Interest in Enigma has not waned with the passing years. The re-opening of Bletchley Park as a museum dedicated to the achievements of World War II codebreakers there, coupled with a Hollywood feature film or two, have kept Enigma in the public eye. This means that when an Enigma machine comes up for sale, it tends to attract a good deal of attention, and a rather impressive price-tag.

You can also buy a millimetre-perfect fully-functioning replica Enigma machine, for about the same price as a corroded one dug out of a river-bed, and you can download for nothing an Enigma simulator to run on your computer. School groups can find tools which use Enigma as a way to discover aspects of mathematics through a historical account of spying on other people's secrets. The Enigma industry is clearly thriving in the Enigma's afterlife, well after its practical use as a communications security device ceased to be. One question remains: what difference did Enigma actually make in its heyday in World War II?

CHAPTER NINE

The final analysis

What, in the end, was the significance of Enigma? How much difference did it make: was the struggle to master Enigma the battle that won World War II? The historian Sir Harry Hinsley, who served for the duration of the war in intelligence at Bletchley Park, should know the answer:

> My own view is that given that the Soviets survived the German attack and the Americans came in as they did, the combined forces of Russia, America and the British would eventually have won the war. The long term relative strengths of Germany and those three countries were such that Germany was bound to lose in the end.... I think we would

have won but it would have been a long and much more brutal and destructive war.

What, then, was the overall influence of intelligence on the war? ... The claim that intelligence by itself won the war – a claim that is self-evidently absurd – may be dismissed.... By how much then did the Allied superiority in intelligence shorten the war?... If the invasion [of continental Europe by the Allies in 1944] had had to be deferred, it might well have been delayed beyond 1946 or 1947 by Germany's V-weapon offensive against the United Kingdom and her ability to finish the Atlantic Wall....

My own calculation is ... the war would have been something like two years longer, perhaps three years longer, possibly four years longer than it was.

These quotations imply, particularly in a context where Sir Harry discussed at length the contribution that Enigma decrypts brought to the overall Allied intelligence picture, that Enigma was significant, possibly very significant indeed. But care is needed. Sir Harry was talking not just about Enigma, but about 'Ultra', and it is Ultra that made the most substantial, if not the only, contribution to the intelligence picture. Ultra was intelligence gleaned from 'Most Secret Sources', or to decode that piece of jargon, from decrypts of coded enemy signals.

We are then left with a slightly difficult job of trying to unpick the contribution of Enigma to Ultra. Ultra was made up from innumerable species of codes and ciphers, of which Enigma was only one. We certainly know that very significant contributions to Ultra came from non-Enigma codes and ciphers.

Innumerable 'hand ciphers' – cipher techniques where letters were transposed or substituted using some scheme or other without the aid of a machine – were unravelled at Bletchley Park. On the whole, hand ciphers are assumed to be simpler to break than machine ciphers, so they tend to be used for carriage of messages of short-term intelligence value. It is probably fine to use an easy-to-break hand cipher to cover the signal 'Implement Plan Alpha at 1159 hours', for by the time the enemy has figured it out it is likely to be too late for them to do much about it; but it would be another matter altogether if an easy-to-read cipher is used for a signal describing Plan Alpha itself.

Still, hand ciphers can be sophisticated and difficult to break; and once they're cracked their security is illusory. Some German units used 'double transposition' ciphers, which are notoriously hard to crack. Transposition means using a scheme, typically a grid of squared paper and an agreed methodology, to rearrange the letters of the original message into a jumble like an enormous anagram. Single transposition is usually breakable by a tedious process of trial-and-error coupled with familiarity of the idiosyncrasies of the language of the message (as with letter frequencies, digraphs come up with predictable frequencies – EN is the most common two-letter combination in German – and patterns can be spotted if the letters of a transposed message are lined up vertically rather than horizontally). Double-transposition is the same thing done twice, usually involving a different jumbling system for each stage of transposition, and makes pattern-spotting very hard. But there were double-transposition experts among the codebreakers.

Then there were codes, where whole words or phrases were coded as four- or five-digit sequences. Rebuilding codebooks was a traditional cryptographic exercise in which all the veteran codebreakers from World War I were familiar. However, security techniques move on, and by World War II the coded phrases were usually disguised by adding another four- or five-digit number chosen from a 'superencipherment' book. The message recipient had to subtract the cipher sequence to reveal the original code sequence, and then look up the meaning of the code in the code-book. If the cipher sequence was changed often enough, or the starting point for the numerical sequences in the superencipherment book were unpredictable, getting to the code sequence could be a difficult task for the codebreaker. Except that machinery, mainly punched-card technology available to all sides in the conflict, was rapidly harnessed to help strip off superencipherments. World War II proved that superenciphered codes were no harder to crack than other types of hand cipher.

One notable example of hand ciphers broken at Bletchley was the ciphers used by the Abwehr, the German military intelligence network. Certainly, some Abwehr operatives used Enigma, as we saw in Chapter 3, but many did not. An organization at Bletchley initially led by World War I army cryptanalyst veteran Oliver Strachey focused on these. It was called ISOS, for 'Illicit Services Oliver Strachey' (compared with ISK, Illicit Services Knox, which tackled the Abwehr's Enigma messages). 'Illicit Services' meant that the radio transmissions were typically being sent by undercover operatives located in places they should not be – in neutral countries or even behind enemy lines. The to-and-fro traffic revealed exactly what German military intelligence knew, didn't know and wanted to know, and that in turn revealed a great deal about the planning of operations and the thinking of the top brass. Towards the end of the war, ISOS was able to build a complete and largely accurate picture of the Germans' own codebreaking organization from ISOS signals with verification from some prisoner-of-war interrogations.

Away from hand ciphers it is also false to imagine that Enigma was the only type of cipher machine in use in the German forces. Numerous other machines were tried, though it has to be admitted that Enigma was the winner for a host of practical reasons. The

The T52 'Sturgeon'.

machine was portable and easy to use. It offered huge security – at least when it was used correctly, with no nonsense like lazy choices of indicator sequences – and versatility. It's no surprise that, once it was embedded across the German armed services, it was virtually impossible to shift them out of using this simple and effective device.

Furthermore, the other types of machinery weren't hugely secure. The Germans experimented for some years with a T52 *Geheimschreiber*, which was an in-line device where the operator typed in the message in plaintext; unlike Enigma, the machine automatically converted the letters into the teleprinter code, enciphered them (using, like Enigma, a rotor system), and transmitted them down a phone line. At the other end a similar machine received the signal, deciphered and printed it. The British named the system 'Sturgeon', since all teleprinter cipher devices were named after fish at Bletchley Park. Largely because Sturgeon was used on land lines rather than radio, the Bletchley Park codebreakers didn't devote much effort to it. But the German security specialists recognized early on that the T52 system was easy to break, and discontinued it on various networks.

A more secure system – at least as perceived by the German security experts – was another form of fish. This one the British called 'Tunny', which in those days was what British folk called tuna. Tunny was the product of a machine whose real name was the Lorenz *Schlüsselzusatz*, meaning cipher attachment. The Lorenz attachment was connected to a regular teleprinter machine, and as with Sturgeon, the operator typed in the message which was automatically enciphered and transmitted. Lorenz messages, however, were commonly sent by radio, which gave the British an opportunity.

Both the T52 and Lorenz teleprinter devices were incredibly bulky and hard to use. When Marshal Kesselring's Lorenz communications team was captured in 1945 it occupied six trucks. There was no way that Lorenz could be a tactical-signals substitute for Enigma, but for high-grade signals of strategic importance between headquarters it was considered to be the best way for the high commands of the German forces to communicate.

Starting in 1942 with a breakthrough by John Tiltman, Bletchley Park poured a huge amount of resource into tackling Tunny. The first step was the reverse-engineering of the Lorenz machine's structure and operational process by the mathematician Bill Tutte, a feat which rivals Marian Rejewski's 1932 attack on Enigma. Huge numbers of Tunny messages could be broken by hand because of errors by the Germans, the most common being to send more than one signal using the same machine settings. Additionally, with effect from 1943 and the arrival of Max Newman (Alan Turing's Cambridge supervisor and lifelong mentor) at Bletchley, machine cryptanalysis was tried, ultimately leading to the development of the electronic Colossus device to find some of the wheel settings used in the Lorenz machine.

Decrypted Tunny messages gave high-level insights into Germany's strategic objectives; being broader in scope the durability of the intelligence gleaned was greater than that from Enigma decrypts. However, it is extremely hard to tell whether a particular operational decision taken by Allied commanders can be attributed to Tunny, or Enigma, or other sources, since the commander saw a product codenamed 'Ultra', which often combined them all.

By looking into the archival files it is possible to get a sense of the volumes of traffic which some of the 'Most Secret Sources' generated. Some files show the name of the 'key' from which the broken message came: colours and bird-names were used for Enigma keys; fish names for teleprinter keys.

Enigma codebreaking in numbers

Number of Enigma messages broken at PC Bruno by the Franco-Polish team in *six months* January-June 1940: 8,440

Number of Enigma messages broken at Bletchley Park on a typical *day* in 1942: 1,995

Number of Bombe machines in the UK in 1945: 210

Snapshot of Enigma codebreaking in February 1942

	intercepted	% decoded
German Air Force messages	31,889	60
All German messages	51,047	41

Some archival files are compendia of decrypts, which survive in huge volumes. Nevertheless, volume is not necessarily indicative of value. Much of the content of decrypted Enigma messages is trivial – it is almost a rarity to find that one signal contained a gem of vital intelligence. Enigma messages were more useful in helping build up an overall picture. Enigma typically provided small items of data, like the dots in a black-and-white newspaper photograph, which should be combined and then viewed from a distance if the picture is to emerge. To be of intelligence value, Enigma codebreaking required database management on a huge scale, something which Bletchley Park was able to imagine and execute, and may even be their most impressive, if under-appreciated, achievement.

Perhaps, to get a sense of the significance of Enigma, we need to start afresh, and look at the course of the war and how Enigma may have influenced a change of direction at different junctures. To begin with, the assault on Enigma was not very successful. Before the Bombe machines began to make their presence felt, the older hand methods of breaking Enigma had to be relied on. The number of messages that could actually be broken this way was small and the results were limited. To quote Sir Harry Hinsley again:

> The Enigma was broken by hand with a delay of several days, sometimes even weeks... its plain language end-product ... presented British intelligence with immense problems in evaluation on account of the intricate procedures, the code-names, the pro-formas and the other conventions which it employed for the sake of brevity or in the interests of internal security – not to speak of the difficulties sometimes created by poor interception and other sources of textual corruption.... For all these reasons high-grade Sigint [signals intelligence] was not flowing regularly from GC and CS to Whitehall until after the outbreak of the Norwegian campaign.

Nevertheless, the techniques were good. Colonel Louis Rivet, the head of French military intelligence, noted in his diary for 10 March 1940, that the decrypts from 'Bruno' were becoming interesting. 'PC Bruno' was the official name of the location just outside Paris to where the joint Franco-Polish codebreaking team had relocated at the beginning of the year. Even after the German air and land forces changed the Enigma indicator procedure in May 1940 valuable intelligence was possible, notably for the Battle of France. To the dismay of the codebreakers, though, the intelligence was wasted. Gustave Bertrand, in command at PC Bruno, was able to furnish the Allied air force command with a complete picture of the Germans' planned aerial bombardment of Paris, codenamed Operation Paula, in early June. The codebreakers had the full details at their fingertips: the strength of the attacking force, the direction of attack, the timing, the works. And nothing was done. Bertrand described the experience as feeding '*confiseries aux cochons*', or sweeties to swine. The fact is, whatever opinions one might hold as to the mettle of Allied commanding air force generals in France in 1940, the commands were not yet receptive to signals intelligence and not yet adapted to revising their appreciations of what was happening in line with its output.

Partly, in Britain and its armed forces, the blindness to the value of Enigma can be attributed to the obsessive desire for secrecy to protect the 'Most Secret Sources'. From January 1940 material derived from decrypts was supplied to military and air intelligence in disguise, pretending that it had come from some all-seeing agent with the cover name BONIFACE. That had the unfortunate effect of downgrading the value of the intelligence to that of other agent-based information, which was often unreliable. It would take a few more campaigns and a lot more experience for reliable routines to be developed, through which senior officers indoctrinated into the Ultra secret could assess for themselves what implications might flow from the signals decrypted at Bletchley Park.

After the fall of France came the great existential threat of an invasion of the British Isles, beginning with the Battle of Britain and the Blitz in the summer and autumn of 1940. The early Bombes were able to produce key solutions leading to German Air Force decrypts during the Battle, though their influence on the decision-making by RAF Fighter Command is hard to gauge. What Enigma decrypts offered was more gradual than immediate in nature: a picture, steadily coming into focus, of the German Air Force's battle-strength and reserves. Based on the Enigma data, British Air Intelligence recognized that it had overestimated the German bomber force at more than double its actual size. Perhaps that gave Air Chief Marshal Dowding the confidence to commit his fighters in a way that would otherwise have seemed rash and dangerous.

Yet the operational history of the first years of the war was one of unbroken success for the German military machine and an almost unbroken series of retreats and withdrawals for the British. Noteworthy among those withdrawals was the loss of Crete in May 1941. Early accounts of this near-disaster give no place to signals intelligence, since its contribution to commanders' thinking remained classified for many decades. Now it seems that Ultra provided a reasonably accurate view of German plans, though some cover-story about a spy in Athens may have been used. If only one intelligence lesson comes out of the failed defence of Crete, it would be that good intelligence is not enough to defeat an invasion.

The campaign in the Western Desert against Rommel and the eventual victory in North Africa marks the pivot-point of signals intelligence, in much the same way that Winston Churchill described the Battle of El Alamein as turning the 'hinge of fate' towards ultimate Allied victory in the war. Enigma decrypts flowed into the hands of the British commanders in Egypt; by the time Montgomery took command the process was smooth, and the volume of decrypts sufficient to build a good intelligence picture. Monty knew that Rommel's supply line was over-extended; the Royal Navy and the RAF exploited knowledge of the sailing patterns of trans-Mediterranean Axis convoys to intercept them and make Rommel's problems even worse. The information came at least partly from Enigma decrypts, and the indoctrination structures were now in place so that appropriate and timely action could be taken based on what was revealed.

By 1942, and the turning-point in North Africa, the war at sea was a pinch-point of vulnerability for Britain owing to the horrific attacks on Allied convoys in the North Atlantic. Mastery of U-boat

Enigma was a vital weapon in that struggle, so that convoys could be routed away from the lurking wolf-packs. By the spring of 1943, Bletchley Park had mastered the four-rotor version of Enigma, and by happy coincidence at this point in the battle the provision of on-board direction-finding and accurate radar for detection of U-boats, together with the availability of air cover across the whole ocean and new anti-submarine weapons, effectively ended the supremacy of the submarines. Perhaps, given the utter dependence of the British war effort on the Atlantic lifeline – not to mention the safety of the American forces crossing over to conduct invasions of North Africa, Sicily and France – the greatest contribution made by Enigma decryption was in this part of the conflict.

As we have seen, after 1942 the Germans turned to other types of machine cipher for their highest-level communications, and the contribution of Enigma might have waned to a degree. This makes the role of Enigma decryption in the runup to the Normandy Landings in June 1944 rather difficult to assess, even though we know that Ultra in general provided a great part of the intelligence picture. By 1944, Bletchley Park's product had matured from a stream of decrypts to an overall intelligence assessment, based on the various sources available to it. Nevertheless, Enigma made its mark on Overlord. German Army Enigma traffic, insofar as it was available, was of little value; by contrast, the German Air Force material helped create that picture built of tiny dots to show the Order of Battle of the German defence; knowing the disposition of units across northern France was crucial to the establishment of a secure bridgehead. Hut 3 provided information on the positions of 58 German divisions in France, Belgium and the Netherlands, together with data on their strengths, commanders and armour.

Furthermore, Enigma played a critical role in ensuring that disposition remained essentially unchanged. At the heart of the

Allies' intention to pin the Germans where they wanted them – a long way away from the Normandy beaches – was the deception plan called Fortitude. The Allies assembled the First US Army Group (FUSAG) under US General George S. Patton, located near the Kent coast. FUSAG was a formidable force, replete with tanks, its own insignia, voluble radio-traffic and all the other trappings of a military organization. Clearly the Americans were going to throw a big punch across the Channel, an uppercut to Calais' chin to follow the belly-blow in Normandy. Except that the tanks were inflatables, the insignia were fake, the radio messages were dummy signals with no content and – apart from the person of General Patton himself – FUSAG did not exist. The challenge was to ensure the Germans believed otherwise. Enigma's role here was in ISK traffic – decrypts of the special Abwehr version of Enigma with multiple turnover notches on its coding rotors – going between Abwehr headquarters and Madrid. Madrid housed the 'controller' of one of Nazi Germany's greatest spies, a Spaniard called Pujol and codenamed 'Garbo' who had infiltrated himself into Britain and set up an espionage network spanning the whole country. From Britain Garbo reported to Madrid on the build-up of FUSAG and other matters of interest to the Abwehr; like FUSAG itself, Garbo's network was entirely fake and the content he fed to his controllers was itself controlled by British intelligence. But ISK decrypts showed that the Abwehr had swallowed the bait.

That Fortitude was working was confirmed from another signals intelligence source – the ability of Bletchley Park to decode the messages sent back to Tokyo from Baron Oshima, the Japanese military attaché in Berlin. Ostensibly, Japanese codebreaking was the province of the Americans, but the division of labour (German material to the British, Japanese to the Americans) was only loosely observed, and the British found that the Berlin-Tokyo messages were a mine of information on German thinking at the uppermost level of the Nazi command. Oshima confirmed that the German Armed Forces Supreme Command believed in FUSAG and the threat to Calais, and had deliberately held back tough defensive Panzer divisions there to meet the challenge. It wasn't Enigma, but it was the confirmation the Allies had been hoping for.

One lesson from the Normandy invasion was far from obvious, and it took a defeat and a near miss to register with the Allied military commanders. By 1944, a great deal had been learned about signals intelligence, on both sides of the conflict. From incredulous beginnings, Allied military commanders had now become dependent on the signals intelligence story to settle their plans. Meanwhile, the Germans had learned a great deal about the value of low-grade coded messages which their own units picked up and decrypted on the spot in combat zones. What was do-able by one side was do-able by the other. Radio silence was a powerful shield. So the venture known as Operation Market Garden, the premature and botched parachute assault on the Rhine bridge at Arnhem, was in part a failure because the signals intelligence picture was less comprehensive than in previous operations; crucial photo-reconnaissance and human intelligence seem to have been disregarded. And a few months later, the last counterattack by Germany through the Ardennes in the Christmas 1944 season took the Allies completely by surprise. Complete radio silence on the German side lulled the Allies into believing that everyone was on holiday: the absence of intelligence was taken to be a positive sign that nothing was happening. As Hut 3 noted,

It is a little startling to find that the Germans had a better knowledge of the U.S. Order of Battle from their Signals Intelligence than we had of the German Order of Battle from Source.

'Source', of course, was Enigma. In fact, it was always the case that the picture was, to some degree, incomplete. Bletchley Park's Hut 6 reported in 1942 that it had difficulty with several Enigma 'keys', where operating practices differed from the normal German military modes of working. This meant that messages sent by various SS units or army administration could not be unravelled without disproportionate effort; further, some keys were not tackled because their content was not going to yield useful product. But these problems are the problems of success: priority has to be given to something, and the volume of material produced by the Enigma decryption factory at Bletchley Park was immense.

The veteran codebreaker Ralph Bennett, who subsequently wrote a handful of books about the contribution of Bletchley Park to the changing course of World War II, noted that 'the combined total [of decrypted signals] for the period January 1944-May 1945 is well over 45,000', and that 'about 25,000 signals were sent from Hut 3 to western commands between the opening of the service to Eisenhower's headquarters in January 1944 and the end of hostilities.' To these numbers one might mention that the Ministry of Defence records in the UK National Archives contain numerous series of decrypted telegrams; to take just one example, File DEFE 3/602, called 'Intelligence from intercepted German, Italian and Japanese communications, WWII', contains facsimiles of 1,139 telegrams from the period 24 May to 1 June 1943; there are dozens of similar files each containing similar volumes of material. Truly, Enigma was a copious source.

CHAPTER TEN

Legacy

The idea behind the Enigma machine was simple and yet powerful. Two essential characteristics defined Arthur Scherbius's vision: a series of rotors which could change a polyalphabetic cipher so often that the traditional codebreaking techniques would be defeated, and an astronomic number of keys, or set-up configurations, so that guesswork or brute force one-by-one trial and error would be doomed from the start. The idea, once seen in those shows in the early 1920s and released into the marketplace, inevitably spawned imitations.

Some of the imitations were brazen rip-offs. Most important among the rip-offs was the British Typex machine, which offered greater security than Enigma but was so close to the German machine in concept and design that it could easily be re-rigged to enable Bletchley Park decipherers to type in raw intercepts and read out plain German messages just as if they were German operators in the field. Other rotor machine variants were more sophisticated. The American SIGABA, also known as the Electric Cipher Machine, copied the Enigma principle of electric current passing through rotors whose changing orientation changed the electric pathway and thus the cipher. SIGABA's clever modification was to randomize the stepping pattern of the coding rotors, using a separate set of rotors for this purpose. SIGABA was never broken – at least not as far as available historical records indicate. Other inventions used rotating parts to change the encipherment pattern but without having electric current coursing through rotors. Perhaps the best known among these is a series of machines invented by the Swedish expert Boris Hagelin, which were brought into use on the Allied side in World War II and continued to be used in various modified versions thereafter; another example is the Lorenz in-line teleprinter code encipherment device which contributed to 'Tunny' intelligence for the Allies.

The Lorenz *Schlüsselzusatz* was a fiendishly complex device which switched each of the five binary components needed to make up a single letter of the alphabet. Although Lorenz machines had rotors, that was about the only similarity to Enigma. Nevertheless, the machine attack on Enigma showed that machine methods might be tried where a paper approach would fail. In an attack on Lorenz, the cryptanalytic machine was going to have to do something much tougher and more delicate than the Bombe did with Enigma. Its job was to compare sequences of binary digits, one derived from the intercepted message, the other from superencipherments derived from five of the coding wheels of the Lorenz machine. Finding the pin-settings on those coding wheels was the goal: and in cases where the two sequences being compared were the same 55 per cent of the time, the correct settings might have been found. Fifty-five per cent is a tiny deviation from randomness, so the counting and comparison would have to be extremely accurate. High-speed electronic counters coupled with photoelectric readers that could scan 5,000 characters a second were the answer – added to which an innovative feature of storing one of the two sequences within the machine improved accuracy and speed still further. The ultimate product was the famous machine we know as Colossus.

Colossus is an unfortunate source of confusion for those who imagine Bletchley Park as being focused on a single source of intelligence, the Enigma. Enigma is so powerful in the popular perception of Bletchley that it is hard to believe that other ciphers, more complex than Enigma, were being successfully tackled (not to mention the other ciphers of huge value but lesser complexity). So an even more modern and technologically sophisticated device like Colossus should, presumably, have been the next phase in the attack on Enigma. Unfortunately, not so; there is no evidence that Colossus was even thought to be a possible solution to Enigma; to reprogram Colossus to tackle Enigma would have been an immense task, and one which was completely pointless given that Bombe technology, which continued to serve the codebreakers for another ten years after the war, did the job well enough.

As with the breaking of the Lorenz machine, partly with the aid of Colossus, on the Allied side, Hagelin's early machines were broken by German codebreakers. Enigma was broken by Allied codebreakers. These successes indicated that rotor-based encryption technology was vulnerable. Already, during the war itself, more sophisticated cipher machines were being deployed for a heightened level of security. The Rockex machine was developed for the British by a Canadian inventor, Pat Bayly, in 1942. Like the Lorenz, its function was to add a random cipher-sequence to teleprinter messages to disguise the text before transmission; a similar machine at the receiver's end would strip off the same sequence. The secret of the machine was in the way it generated a pseudo-random sequence which would never be repeated, unlike with rotor-based machines. Rockex became the standard for British secret communications after the war.

But with more complex encryption methods came the danger of more sophisticated decryption. Enigma had shown the way, with the large-scale deployment of Bombes to produce intelligence. With the number of Enigma decrypts mounting to the thousands every single day, Commander Travis, by now the Deputy Director – Services (the director being C, the head of MI6, and the other deputy director being Alastair Denniston, moved sideways to be Deputy Director – Civil, meaning he looked after diplomatic codebreaking) and head of Bletchley Park, established a Machine Coordination and Development Committee in 1943. The Committee looked at all sorts of mechanical issues facing Bletchley Park, from the production and maintenance of Bombes, prioritization of tasks for the punched-card section, availability of Typex machines for deciphering and the all-important attack on Tunny through various experimental machines culminating in Colossus.

It would be wrong to regard Colossus as the progeny of the Bombe, but the confidence gained at Bletchley Park from the success of the Bombe enterprise made the brave step to rely on electronics and even to attempt to find tiny deviations from randomness something worth trying. Machinery was becoming more versatile, and bordering on the fully programmable. Bletchley Park is right to regard itself as a birthplace of modern computing. Things had moved a long way from 1940, when 'computers' were people who sat by adding machines monotonously ploughing through arithmetical calculations, and in a spirit of secrecy the head of Bletchley Park's air section could send a minute saying that 'the Air Ministry have already instituted the use of the word "Computor" in all cases in lieu of "Cryptographer".'

Indeed, the plans for development of programmable electronic computers in the post-war period demanded the recruitment of many former Bletchley Park experts: notable among them were Alan Turing, who went on to design the ACE machine for the National Physical Laboratory, and M.H.A. Newman, who became the professor overseeing the Computing Machine Laboratory at Manchester University. In the United States, the links between computer development and codebreaking are perhaps more tenuous, but they exist, since an ecosystem developed on the East Coast connecting the various military establishments needing computing power, Bell Labs, Princeton University and a seasoning of former signals-intelligence specialists including American alumni of Bletchley Park.

Computers as we now know them began, then, as one tool to facilitate the industrialization of codebreaking, and continue to play a role in cryptanalysis right through to present times. Sometimes, the largest and most powerful computers in the world have been acquired by agencies such as the NSA and GCHQ in order to simplify the process of crunching through permutations and uncover the secrets of potentially hostile powers.

Alongside the development of more secure methods of encryption and more powerful computers for decryption, the authorities have become more nervous about unreadable signals. Following a 2016 case where the Apple Corporation declined to unlock the iPhone of a suspected murderer, legislation called the Lawful Access to Encrypted Data Act was introduced into the US Congress which would make it obligatory for encryption to be unlocked for law enforcement agencies. This is simply another step on a road whereby US authorities have sought to control the use of codes and ciphers so as to keep the degree of security within the bounds of what the NSA can easily observe.

The timeline of development of secure encryption techniques for everyday use approximates to that of the growth of the internet

The NSA's Cray supercomputer from 1976.

as a commercial medium and the need for citizens to communicate personal or financial information securely. But interest in codes and ciphers among the general public probably started some years before the internet. A landmark in that history was the publication in 1967 by the American historian Dr David Kahn of his seminal book *The Codebreakers*. Weighing in at around 1.5kg (3.3 pounds) and 1,000 pages, this was the first thorough account of the history of codebreaking. The coverage of World War II was all the more remarkable because it focused on the German attacks on Allied codes, and there was barely a mention of the now famous achievements of the Allies, and no discussion whatever of the solution of Enigma. In 1967, all that was still secret. Since then everything has changed. The German successes have been almost completely forgotten, and Enigma is centre-stage, with all spotlights trained upon it so brightly that even other Allied achievements cannot be seen in the shadows alongside. Coupled with the excitement generated by the use of early machine techniques for decryption, the scale of the attack on Enigma and its success have built up the legend of Enigma into a saga of epic proportions in the public consciousness. As John Ferris, the historian appointed to write the centenary-year official history of GCHQ, has said, Bletchley Park's contribution to World War II is often overstated by the public. But Professor Ferris's book is itself called *Behind the Enigma*, showing just how immoveable the Enigma machine has become in the perception of GCHQ's history of achievement.

A less breathless analysis than headline-writers might favour points to a lasting, and important, legacy of Enigma. It might be found in the overlapping histories of computer development and signals-intelligence organization.

The codebreaking of Enigma was based on a paradigm shift in the way codebreakers approached their craft. The volume of material generated from Enigma decrypts would not have been possible if they had stuck to their old methods using pencils and paper, however imaginative and sophisticated their ideas. Using machines to take out much of the drudgery of sifting out impossible machine settings became the way forward; it was not just Enigma which relied on machinery as a cryptanalytic aid. Punched-card technology was deployed at Bletchley Park in substantial quantities, with large numbers of dedicated staff and its own building and sub-organization. The punched card machines worked on Enigma as well as superenciphered codebooks, code generation and, occasionally, highly complex analytical processes requiring the creation of special algorithms to solve one-off problems. Computers as we now know them began, then, as one tool to facilitate the industrialization of codebreaking, and continue to play a role in cryptanalysis right through to present times.

In the structure and organization of codebreaking agencies can be seen another significant legacy of Enigma codebreaking. In the earliest days of World War II, before any Enigma product was anything more than imaginary, one of the future stars of Bletchley Park went to his boss with an idea. The star was Gordon Welchman, and the vision he had was ambitious, bordering on arrogant, and completely fantastic. The boss was Commander Travis, and the idea was the 'Hut system' described in chapter 4. At a time when the flow of Enigma decrypts was not yet even a trickle, the idea was crazy. Crazy, yet Travis agreed.

Even after the war was over, Welchman continued to argue passionately for good organization in signals intelligence. Some of the errors and oversights towards the end of the war could be attributed to weakness in organization. The problem is complex. The issue is that the product, its provenance, and its process, are all highly secret, so nobody knows or trusts the god-like pronouncements of those in the know; discipline in use of the secret product is hard to enforce. This goes for both the secrecy of one's own communications as much as the interpretation of intelligence based on one's opponent's communications. In writing his own account of Bletchley Park, *The Hut Six Story*, in the early 1980s, Welchman devoted four chapters to 'Today' and the ongoing lessons which should be drawn from the Enigma experience at Bletchley Park. In the prologue to his book, he says:

> Whereas years earlier I had been involved in breaking down the security of the German communications system, now my task was to protect the security, and also the survivability, of our new battlefield communications systems.... Thus, in telling the story of Hut 6, I have emphasized those aspects of clandestine activities that are still relevant....
>
> I am convinced that the Hut 6 story can contribute to this planning. The principle of the bombe, a completely new electro-mechanical device that we built to help us break the Enigma, should have been made known many years ago; it contains a clear warning, much needed today, that our confidence in cryptographic security should not depend solely on the number of possibilities an enemy cryptanalyst must examine to break a code, and on the assumption that he must examine each possibility individually.

These wise words from Gordon Welchman are one of Enigma's most important legacies. Today, more than ever before, we depend on security of communications for all aspects of our lives. It is not just about keeping our mobile phone-calls and emails private, but about everything from the hacking of credit card details to the integrity of public infrastructure. Cryptographic systems in use today are older than Enigma was in the middle of World War II. New cryptanalytic techniques, in the form of quantum computing, are just around the corner. Indeed, understanding Enigma can help us all with our security. Security, disclosure of cryptological secrets, declassification and publicity are also part of the legacy of Enigma. As Gordon Welchman knew well, having been vilified for publishing details of Enigma codebreaking 40 years after it was a live secret, the story of Enigma was itself wrapped in layers of secrecy for many decades. The veterans of Bletchley Park were forbidden by law to divulge the slightest hint of what they knew.

Notwithstanding the strictures, there were so many slips and disclosures by the early 1970s that investigative journalists and others had fastened on to a potential scoop. It began with a page or two in a book published in Poland in 1967, in which the Polish military historian Władysław Kozaczuk revealed that Polish codebreakers had cracked the Enigma before the start of World War II. But, in the West, nobody had much access to Polish historical literature and few people spoke Polish. France, however, was a different matter. Spurred by a write-up of the intelligence story of the war which he thought unfair and wrong, Gustave Bertrand wrote a full-length book which told the full story of Enigma based on his contemporary documents, up to the time of the total occupation of France in late 1942. Being a retired officer whose post-war career had been spent in the French signals intelligence agency, Bertrand knew better than to tell too much, so he stopped short of describing the activities of Bletchley Park or the attack on Enigma using Bombes. But France and its literature were well within reach of British writers. One or two veterans of the war were itching to share their stories, faint sketches appeared in some memoirs, and suddenly the risk of a full, unauthorized, and possibly damaging disclosure was present.

By 1974, the UK government appreciated that the position was untenable and, judiciously or otherwise, allowed the publication of a book called *The Ultra Secret* by F.W. Winterbotham, followed by an official history called *British Intelligence in World War II*. These books disclosed not only the existence of Bletchley Park (the existence of GCHQ itself being supposedly still a secret) but also Bletchley's wartime success against Enigma. Yet, a few years on, it was still possible for people like Gordon Welchman to be censured for disclosing some of the details of *how* Enigma had been broken – even in the early 1980s that was considered information too sensitive for anyone to know, despite the fact that nobody had been breaking operational Enigma messages for nearly 30 years.

The authorized story of Enigma codebreaking in the official history did not, unhappily for the secrecy-minded British Government, complete the picture. Rather, it conjured into existence a vast pool of public inquisitiveness about what was seen as a terrific World War II story, combining a revision of strategic and tactical decision-making, the triumph of brains over bloodshed, and a big question about communications security in the present day which has not been resolved.

It also created a subcultural industry of myths and legends. Winterbotham's book contained not just the canard of the Coventry bombing decision and a hilariously inaccurate description of the Bombe machine, but a catalogue of other errors of interpretation and mistaken recollection.

A Polish mechanic had been employed in a factory in Eastern Germany ... was sacked and sent back to Poland ... and got in touch with our [British] man in Warsaw... In due course the young Pole was persuaded to leave Warsaw and was secretly smuggled out under a false passport with the help of the Polish

Secret Service; he was then installed in Paris where ... he began to make a wooden mock-up of the machine he had been working on in Germany.

The official history, being a much more solidly-founded work, cannot be accused in quite the same way, but its initial effort at an account of the first attack on Enigma was not based on good sources and contained its own mistakes:

> On the work of the Polish mathematicians the Polish accounts provide the following further information... From 1934, greatly helped by a Pole who was working in an Enigma factory in Germany, they began to make their own Enigma machines. However, these were crude and time-consuming, and it was only later that they developed mechanical versions of the Enigma machine.

This nonsense was published in 1979, when Marian Rejewski alone of the Polish mathematical codebreakers was still alive. Rather politely, Rejewski – then in retirement and well into his seventies – published a corrective commentary. Nevertheless, one of the lasting consequences of the errors in the official history has been a sense of grievance among Poles that their own crucial national contribution was officially whitewashed out of the history books.

It is not just in non-fiction that strange Enigma stories can be found. As well as Robert Harris's book *Enigma*, which was made into a Hollywood film starring Dougray Scott and Kate Winslet as mentioned in Chapter 3, there have been numerous novels inspired by the Enigma machine or the effort to break Enigma at Bletchley Park. There have also been stage plays and television series. Enigma acts powerfully on the imagination and people enjoy the link to the place, and the Enigma story, that has become instantly recognizable and a source of national pride. Some are detective stories or mysteries; some, like Agatha Christie's book featuring 'Major Bletchley' are only loosely associated with the site, even if rather fun; some are just weird. An internet list 'based on recommendations by thought leaders and experts' of the 16 'Best Enigma Machine Books of All Time' has, in fact, only one book devoted exclusively to Enigma cryptanalysis; of the others, ten cover cryptology generally, specific episodes in the Enigma story, or Bletchley Park, two are Alan Turing biographies (illustrating how his story is somehow perceived to equate to the story of Enigma), one is a novel, one is a puzzle book, and one has absolutely no content whatever, being a blank-pages notebook which 'awaits your writing pleasure'.

Truth can, indeed, be stranger than fiction; even in a blank-pages notebook it would be hard to make this one up. It was a Saturday in April 2000 at Bletchley Park. The Park had been attempting for several years to survive as a museum, the cost of saving the site from bulldozers being a monumental struggle for financial survival. On that fateful Saturday one of the museum's precious Enigma machines – an Abwehr four-rotor model – had disappeared from its display stand. In those days, security at the museum was weak, since there just weren't the resources to provide full protection. Had it just been moved by an officious volunteer? Or was something more sinister afoot?

The machine could not be found; the unavoidable conclusion was that the museum was the victim of theft. Then ransom notes began to arrive. Suitably enough, the sender encoded his name for greater anonymity. The Bletchley Park Trust was to pay up £25,000 for the return of the machine. There was not the faintest chance that they could lay hands on that sum, but a sting operation might be possible instead.

The ransom money of £25,000 was due to be handed over in a graveyard. Police hunched behind gravestones on a damp October afternoon in Derbyshire. But someone got suspicious and the handover failed. The director of the museum was threatened with the destruction of the machine; the museum staff and volunteers were getting nervous about their own personal safety. It was all getting rather too melodramatic. Then, a few days later, the museum's phone rang. The caller was Jeremy Paxman, the celebrated broadcaster, who had received a rather curious parcel – an Abwehr four-rotor Enigma machine, albeit without three of its rotors.

It was, in the end, a case of all's well that ends reasonably well. In September 2001 one of the conspirators, who had written the ransom notes, pleaded guilty at Aylesbury Crown Court to charges of blackmail and handling stolen goods; the theft itself had been motivated by discontent on the board of the Trust. Eventually the machine was returned, and the missing rotors handed over in the less dramatic setting of a motorway service area.

Nowadays, the Bletchley Park Trust is on a much sounder financial footing, attracting around 250,000 visitors a year to see where World War II codebreaking actually happened, and to learn the ins and outs of Enigma codebreaking. Next door, at The National Museum of Computing, a rebuilt Bombe machine is demonstrated regularly to the public and its functions explained. Its place there neatly positions the Bombe in the historical timeline of proto-computers, so that visitors can trace the development of computing machinery, via Colossus, to modern programmable electronic devices.

Both museums run engaging courses and education programmes for schools and other groups. Enigma is a key part of the narrative: students can develop mathematical skills by solving codebreaking puzzles structured around Enigma while able to engage with a real Enigma machine. It's a field day doing mathematics in a way which surprises and stretches the imagination. Perhaps Enigma's ability to enthuse and to teach people about all sorts of questions in fields extending well beyond codebreaking is its lasting, and most important legacy.

Bibliography

Alan Turing: The Enigma by Andrew Hodges (Simon & Schuster, 1983)

Dilly – The Man Who Broke Enigmas by Mavis Batey (Dialogue, 2009)

Intercept: The Secret History of Computers and Spies by Gordon Corera (Orion Publishing, 2016)

Alan Turing Decoded: the man they called Prof by Dermot Turing (The History Press, 2021)

The Bombe by Dermot Turing (Arcturus Publishing, 2021)

The Debs of Bletchley Park by Michael Smith (Aurum Press, 2015)

The Hut Six Story by Gordon Welchman (Allen Lane, 1982)

The Secrets of Station X by Michael Smith (Biteback Publishing, 2011)

The Ultra Secret by F. W. Winterbotham (Weidenfeld & Nicolson, 1974)

X, Y and Z – the real story of how Enigma was broken by Dermot Turing (The History Press, 2018)

Index

Picture Credits

Alamy: 32, 44, 48, 115
Bletchley Park Trust: 141
Crypto Museum: 186, 191
GCHQ: 75, 154
Geoffrey Pidgeon: 130
Getty Images: 105
Józef Piłsudski Institute: 41
King's College, Cambridge: 81
National Cryptologic Museum: 171
Public Domain: 16, 25, 60, 66
Service historique de la Défense: 36
Shutterstock: 78
The National Archives, UK: 14, 59, 85
Wikimedia Commons: 34, 99, 112, 113, 148, 178, 189, 207, 224
William McElhinney: 21, 89, 99